Darlington Memories

The publishers would like to thank the following companies for their

support in the production of this book

Main Sponsor

Bussey & Armstrong

Amdega

Darlington Club & Institute

Darlington Abbeyfield Society

William Dodds

Dolphin Centre

Alan H Goodrick

The Leas Bakery

North View Engineering Limited

John Wade (Haulage) Limited

Henry Williams

First published in Great Britain by True North Books Limited
England HX5 9AE
01422 377977

ISBN 1 903204 46 1

Text, design and origination by True North Books Limited
Printed and bound by The Amadeus Press Limited

Darlington Memories

Contents

Introduction

Once upon a time in Darlington there was no colour television; indeed not so long ago there was no television at all, let alone video recorders, walkmans and personal computers. Nor was there central heating to keep us warm; in winter frost flowers would cover our bedroom windows. We would melt a hole through the ice with hot pennies (big ones, not today's tiny decimal tiddlers) to make a peep-hole through the glass. Whatever happened to that Darlington?

The name of Darlington is world famous. It's a name which is engraved in every historian's heart as being one end of the renowned Stockton-Darlington railway which in 1825 carried us into the modern age.

This book is designed to help those who want to recall the days of the not so distant past, days which are within the memory of not only the very oldest, who can recall the Great War of 1914-18 but those who are younger too, those who lived through the second world war and those who are only now just beginning to realise that their early lives too are already becoming part of history: the rock and roll years of the 1950s, the swinging sixties with mini skirts and scooters, mods and rockers, the Beatles and the Rolling Stones. Even the 1970s and 80s are now decades ago, even though for many the events like the miners' strike and the Thatcher government still seem as if they happened only yesterday.

But where did today's Darlington come from? Evidence for the existence of a settlement on the site of the present town is first found in Saxon times. A 7th century Saxon cemetery was found in 1876 on the Greenbank estate near Dodd Street. It is doubtful though that those early settlers would have recognised the town's name today, even if the name is a Saxon one. At the time of the Norman conquest the settlement was Dearthington and a century later variously Dearnington and Dirlington. The origin of the name is uncertain though some suggest that it had its beginnings as the settlement of

Families enjoying the roller blading facilities in South Park.

Deornup's people. Sadly one thing we do not have is a reference in the Domesday Book of 1086 which stops short of the River Tees.

In the 10th century the coffin of St Cuthbert rested in Darlington before being taken by monks to Chester-le-Street, an event commemorated by the present Church of St Cuthbert. The great marketplace bounded by Headrow, Tubwell Row, Horsemarket and St Cuthbert's churchyard was probably laid out around 1164 when Bishop Hugh Pudsey built a manor house beside the Skerne.

By the 14th century wealthy Darlington wool merchants were exporting bales of wool to Flanders via the port of Newcastle as well as being involved in weaving, fulling and dyeing woollen cloth. By 1380 Darlington was by far the wealthiest amongst the neighbouring boroughs of Gateshead, Sunderland and Durham.

In 1585 a terrible fire swept through the town destroying 273 houses. High Row and Skinnergate were gutted and 80 people made homeless. The only buildings to survive the Tudor period were in the lower part of the town. The last remaining example of those buildings, The Nags Head in Tubwell Row and originally the vicarage, was demolished in the 1960s - all except for a rear wall which was incorporated into the rebuilt pub. But the wool trade was already declining by the time of the great fire; leather workers by then were outnumbering weavers with the linen industry growing in importance.

Perhaps one of the best remembered incidents in Darlington's history however was the visit to the town in 1617 by James I. He stayed at the Crown Inn and whilst there commented 'Darnton! I think it is Darnton i't dirt'. Fortunately the town has been cleaned since then.

Despite the dirt, by the mid 18th century the town's population had grown to over 3,000 and with the re-emergence of the woollen textiles industry it would rise to over 5,000 in 1801.

The advent of that famous railway increased the population still further. Terraced housing grew northwards towards the station and railway works, whilst the coming of iron and engineering industries led to building eastwards to Bank Top and Albert Hill. By the mid 19th century the plots behind High Row, Skinnergate, Tubwell Row, Bondgate and Northgate had been filled up with courts and yards. From the 1870s the fine terraces of large Victorian and Edwardian houses would appear to the south and west of the town centre and beyond them impressive mansions reflecting the town's increasing prosperity. By 1901 and the

A busy scene on Northgate in the mid 1960s.

death of Queen Victoria the population of the once small Saxon settlement had grown to almost 50,000.

No-one is alive today to tell us first hand of those long ago events though many of the buildings from the Victorian era, and not a few from even earlier, survive as living testaments to the enterprise and ingenuity of our forbears.

We may not recall the building of such ancient edifices but many readers will recall more recent construction work such as the Darlington Inner Ring Road, approved in 1952 and constructed in stages. To make way for the new road property was demolished beyond the River Skerne, behind Northgate and Bondgate and along one side of Victoria Road. The Borough Council built St Cuthbert's way and St Augustine's way between 1969 and 1974. Following a public enquiry in 1990 it was decided to suspend plans to build the last section. The line of the ring road however roughly defines the boundary of the old medieval town with the market Place at its heart and Northgate, Blackwellgate, Tubwell Row and Bondgate radiating from it.

But it is our more recent history, our personal history, that this book, Darlington Memories, celebrates with its evocative pictures and informative text reminding us of events that we never want to forget. There are happy times and times, festivals and celebrations contrasted with war and hardship. Our working lives as well as our playtime are given unique coverage each offering up both small and large reminders of events we had almost begun to forget. If you can remember sitting in front of a glowing coal fire to listen to the Home Service or to Children's Hour on the wireless, or if you can recall the voice of Lord Haw Haw calling from Germany or food rationing then this is the book for you. And if you are younger still then can you recall going to school in the 1950s, 60s and even 70s? Can you remember all those endless crazes from hula-hoops to clackers?

This extraordinary record of life as it was lived in Darlington during the 20th century is a book which will be treasured by all who read it. It is a book which will be valued not only for the pleasure it will give each individual reader but for the opportunity it will provide, now and in the future, for mothers and fathers, grandmothers and grandfathers to remind each other of events of yesteryear and to share their own intensely personal recollections with generations still growing up in our marvellous town. Find a comfy armchair, sit back and enjoy the sheer luxury of pure undiluted nostalgia.

Street scenes

A summer's day in the early 1950s looking north along High Row. It's ten to three and time for tea according to the clock. The Old Town Hall, the Covered Market and the famous Clock Tower were all designed by the famed architect Alfred Waterhouse, who also designed the Natural History Museum in London and Manchester's Town Hall. The building was completed in 1864, the clock itself being a gift from Joseph Pease whose statue, facing us in the far distance, appears to be surrounded by a crowd of loitering pedestrians.

The sun is shining strongly on this warm afternoon, clearly evidenced by the driver of the open topped tourer going away from us and enjoying the summer whilst he can.

Summers were of course far warmer back then or so it seems, the sun always melted the tar on the roads enough for us to get it on our hands and knees, not to mention our clothes, which would drive mother mad when we retuned home, filthy but happy.

Much has changed in the intervening years; if we wanted to recreate this scene we might borrow a fleet of old cars and park them in similar locations but we would find it far harder to put back the trolley bus cables and absolutely impossible to put back the buildings which now form the modern Cornmill shopping centre.

But would we want to go back? The answer for many is yes; back to that innocent age when a microchip was still something you ate!

It is the mid 1950s in this photo, taken from behind the Joseph Pease statue and looking south down High Row. Despite the large number of cars, all parked at 45 degrees, and the vehicles in the distance coming towards us, it is a remarkably quiet scene. Dominating the centre of the picture is the Clock Tower which Joseph Pease gazes at in perpetuity; or almost in perpetuity, he has moved around a little since this picture was taken, moved to greater safety closer to the No Entry sign in the middle ground of the picture. The stone troughs, with flowers in them, at the base of the statue were replaced by concrete tubs when the road improvements were made. These are the days when the second world war

seemed like only yesterday and rock and roll and teddy boys were not yet the stuff of legend. Elvis was still a brash young singer, hardly heard of outside the USA, and those who had heard him and Bill Haley and the Comets could never have guessed in their wildest dreams that pop music would one day become, not only a major industry but a deeply rooted part of western culture. The trolley bus cables, removed in 1958, are clearly visible overhead; how many older readers miss the whine of the trolley buses as they made their way through the town? The cables were an eyesore but those environmentally friendly vehicles didn't belch out diesel fumes in the way their successors did.

Above: Here we are in the early 1960s looking west towards Bondgate. On the far left, with its striped awning, is Swaledale Cleaners, and next to it, dominating the centre of the photograph, is Pearl Assurance House.

The busy junction of Bondgate and High Row at Prospect Place has seen a seemingly endless series of changes over the years to improve traffic flow.

Many readers will still recall the days when the road surface was cobbled, not to mention the installation of the zebra crossing, which in this photo has been moved back from the junction by several yards from its original position in the interests of improved safety. The statue of Joseph Pease in the bottom left hand corner of the scene had recently been moved from its earlier location in the middle of the road junction.

There its plinth formed a mini roundabout; a small pedestrian island, just out of view at the bottom of the scene, was placed on the statue's original site. Though the junction is ancient the view is very much a modern one, even though decades have passed since it was taken. The second world war had long since ended and recognisably modern cars and buses are on the streets.

Top: The name Odeon comes from the Greek theatre of classical times. But the Odeon cinema in Darlington, pictured here in the 1950s, doesn't go back quite that far. Originally the Majestic cinema, this picture palace in Bondgate was opened in 1932 and was renamed the Odeon in 1943 in the midst of the second world war. Despite a major facelift in 1968 audiences were falling

dramatically, as they were in all cinemas under the onslaught of television. Organ recitals were brought back in 1974 in a vain bid to boost attendances alongside all-night films and other novelties. But it was to no avail; the Odeon closed in 1981, the premises reopening five years later as a snooker hall.

It is quite astonishing just how many cinemas Darlington once had. Do you recall the New Empire, the Electric Picture palace, the Court Kinema, the People's Palace and the Scala? It is over a century ago that the first moving pictures were shown in Darlington: in January 1901 the Edison Animated Photo Company set up in the Central Hall which eventually became the town's first permanent cinema showing the silent moves of Charlie Chaplin Buster Keaton and the Keystone Cops. Few today still recall the days of silent films, but many readers will recollect seeing some of the great epics here such as Ben Hur and the Ten Commandments or musicals such as My Fair Lady.

Alas the days of cinemas with ashtrays, wooden spoons for ice-cream tubs and kissing on the back row on a Saturday night have gone forever.

Bottom: The Imperial Hotel is pictured here in March 1972. To mark his year as Mayor of Darlington in 1884 Arthur Pease, who was then also president of the local Temperance Association, had this large hotel built, which was then known as the 'Trevelyan Temperance Hotel', to cater for the needs of the non-drinking traveller. Temperance did not last long however. Improvements to the building were made in 1891-2 and a full licence to sell intoxicating liquor was granted to a new owner, Mr Edward Wooler, who changed the name to the Imperial Hotel.

Edward Wooler ran the Imperial for more than thirty years before selling it to a Miss S P Parsons in 1926. The building was of some architectural interest and in August 1937 a protection order was made on the hotel which was then sold to Darlington Trust Ltd. The hotel was sold yet again, in 1948, to Beverly Bros. Ltd. of Eagle Brewery.

Closure was announced in 1975 with Darlington Council then planning to turn the building into a block of bed-sitters. The bar was re-opened in 1978 as the New Imperial however and optimistic plans to develop the Imperial as a nightspot were announced.

A new bar opened in 1983. Before then however, in 1981, Space City opened an amusement arcade in part of the former hotel. In 1984 the first floor became an antiques centre containing 12 shops, a coffee stall and offices whilst the Imperial Bar re-opened once again in 1988 after a further face-lift.

Below right: Here we are looking down on the intersection of Bondgate and High Row. The vehicles suggest the mid 1960s with a quite modern looking single-decker bus being followed by one of far older vintage, whilst the cars on view on the right, with their headlamps yet to be enclosed within the mudguards, immediately send our thoughts backwards in time. On the far left, just passing the statue of Joseph Pease is a

signpost to the future, a car, possibly a Hillman, which isn't painted black or grey.

Shops in the area clearly visible include Charles, Hintons grocery store and Fleets which had previously been Ridings. Another giveaway of the date of this photograph is the 'street furniture'; traffic lights, No Entry signs and the Belisha beacon. The keep left bollards under the traffic lights seem modern enough but the black and white pole in which the lights sit now looks particularly dated.

Belisha beacons, those orange globes on top of black and white poles, were introduced by Leslie Hore Belisha, the Minster of Transport, in 1934. Between the two world wars an unbelievable 120,00 people had been killed on Britain's roads and this was one way to try and help cut the carnage. In recent years most crossings of this kind have been replaced by Pelican crossings which demand, rather than simply suggest, that drivers should stop to give way to pedestrians - though judging by the volume of traffic in this picture it doesn't look as if many drivers will be likely to go careering over the crossing at top speed.

This photograph of the north side of Duke Street was, we believe, taken in the summer of 1962. The scene has changed somewhat over the intervening years but here, preserved for posterity, are the businesses which then occupied this section of the street from the accountant's office on the far left along to Seaton's, selling cigarettes and confectionery, in the centre and further along the row is an engravers business.

What is remarkable about this photo is the parked vehicles which show the dramatic change in car design which occurred in just a few short years. Though designs had been changing throughout the 1950s the old black pre-war cars symbolised by Ford's 'Tin Lizzy'

had still dominated our roads, and in that era of post-war austerity had been made to last even if we would have liked to trade them in for something a little more modern. And suddenly here is the modern era, not a running board or a mudguard mounted headlight in sight. The man in the far distance walking his tiny dog is perhaps looking at the scene and asking himself where is it all going to end with these new fangled cars and pop music from groups like the Beatles with their mops of hair spilling out from the Light Programme. And that reckless, if handsome, young fellow Kennedy having been elected to the presidency of the USA in 1960, where was he going? Was he about to start the third world war over his dispute with Cuba?

Events & occasions

This patriotic looking photograph, dated 9th February 1952, records the proclamation of the ascension of Queen Elizabeth II being read from the steps of Darlington's Market Hall. Everyone wants to be in on the action with civic dignitaries wearing their ceremonial clothing crowding the steps. In Churchill's words we had entered a new Elizabethan age - though we hoped that there would be no new Spanish Armada to make the reign of the second Elizabeth as memorable as the first. Patriotism was then still a matter of pride. The Union Jack was still a symbol of genuine faith in Britain, its joining of the flags of England, Scotland and Ireland has been part of our heritage since the Act of Union with Ireland in 1801, though an earlier version combining the flags of St George and St Andrew had been in use since the reign of James I, after whom the Jack is said to take its name. Who, in 1952, would have predicted the creation of a Scottish parliament during our new queen's reign?

And what a long reign it would turn out to be. Many of those gazing up at the great and the good would have been born in the reign of Queen Victoria and already lived through the reigns of the four succeeding kings. Whilst the death of the Queen's father was a tragedy for her, for the nation it was a blessing giving a still war weary Britain a symbol of renewal in the form of a young, energetic and attractive monarch who would lead us into the unknown future with hope in our hearts.

Thousands lined the streets of Darlington on 6th May 1935 to celebrate the Silver Jubilee of King George V, brass bands paraded through Darlington flags waving to honour the occasion. Those who were not in uniform could however still parade in their Sunday best with bowler hats and best flat caps. 'Get ahead get a hat' said a somewhat later advertising slogan, but no such advertising jingle was needed back in 1935; going without something on one's head was to be incompletely dressed. Not until the 1960s did head coverings begin to fall out of favour.

To our minds today hats and caps would hardly be necessary, the 6th May was a warm and sunny Spring day and these days would bring out shorts and T-shirts; but not so back then when even a holiday was still a formal occasion requiring best clothes to be put on display. Little did those crowds appreciate just how little there would be to celebrate over the course of the next ten years. We would shortly have another king, the ill-fated Edward who would abdicate over his affections for Mrs Simpson, and in turn the unexpected succession of his brother George who would stoically see us through the war years. At the time of this photograph war was still far from people's minds, even though Hitler in Germany and Mussolini in Italy were already in power and eager to fight someone, the Italians were in what we then still called Abyssinia and the Germans would soon prepare to support France's forces in Spain, testing their Condor Legion of bombers in anticipation of even worse use to come.

Here we are in Skinnergate witnessing the dressing up of the town to celebrate the Silver Jubilee of the reign of George V, our own Queen Elizabeth's grandfather. The date is 6th May 1935 and the bunting is in evidence from every building. George was born in 1865 and was Edward VII's second son, only becoming heir following the untimely death of his elder brother, the Duke of Clarence. George V and his wife Queen Mary were crowned in 1911 after Edward VII's death in 1910. For some the celebrations were tinged with sadness, the King was now 70 years old and would not live long; and others worried that his successor, the playboy Prince of Wales, though a popular figure might prove an ineffectual monarch. For most however the Jubilee was simply a chance to celebrate.

There would be more than a few glasses of Tower Ales sunk to celebrate the monarch's 25 years on the throne; and if one too many glasses were drunk it seemed to matter less back then, one might go rolling home rather worse for wear having made too many patriotic toasts with little fear of being run over by the traffic; Skinnergate in 1935 was virtually empty of cars and vans and the lady stepping out into the roadway and glancing in our direction is more likely to be looking down to make sure she doesn't tread in anything unpleasant in her path than from side to side to check for cars.

Below: No you don't need to get your eyes tested. Despite appearances this isn't Winston Churchill. The lady pictured giving Churchill's famous 'V' for Victory sign with both hands is Maud Fawbert the wife of local legend Geordie Fawbert. Geordie once sold fish on Darlington Market giving rise to the rather slanderous Darlington nursery rhyme popular until the 1950s:

Geordie Fawbert he sells fish,
For three ha'pence it'll make a tasty dish.
But don't buy it, don't buy it,
It smells when you fry it.

Maud was born in the last year of the 19th century and was in her mid 40s when this photograph was taken at the end of the war, participating in the VE day celebrations which were held when the war against Germany was won. Like her husband, Maud Fawbert was a colourful character and was a regular trader on the market wheeling loads of fish from Bank Top station in her own cart.

Quite what significance the Dutch 'boy' and girl have to the picture we do not know though we can guess that they have been dragged away from a pageant of all European nations. Maud has done a perfect job of imitating Winston even down to the trademark cigar clamped in her mouth. Whether the cigar is lit is unclear, probably not, but we bet the fag being carried by the girl on the left is lit, and in those days probably un-tipped too perhaps it's a Wild 'un - or a Woodbine for those too young to recall the nickname.

This photograph from 1920 of the Royal Show, in Darlington, features the Prince of Wales in attendance, his chauffer driven open-topped car making its way carefully through the thronging crowds. The playboy prince was an immensely popular figure especially amongst the young who admired his fashionable choice of dress though, since he is wearing a top hat, he seems to have abandoned sartorial innovation for

this special occasion. Who amongst the crowds that day could have predicted that just 16 years later, as the new King Edward VIII, he would have plunged Britain into a constitutional crisis over his love for the divorced American Wallace Simpson? On this day there were no such fears for the future, the Great War had ended just two years previously and a short-lived economic boom was underway. Now was time for Darlington to celebrate, not worry about tomorrow.

The Royal Shows had been a Darlington institution since the late 19th century when they were founded by Arthur Pease. The very first Show being held at Hummersnott, the Pease mansion, which attracted not only a crowd of 100,000 but also the Shah of Persia the Shazada of Afghanistan and our very own Duke and Duchess of York.

How many readers recall attending a Royal Show?

Perhaps we recall first attending as small children faced for the first time with a forest of legs, thousands of visitors milling around and making we tiny folk demand to be lifted onto father's shoulders to get a better look. How many towns children got their first close up look at cows, pigs and sheep on show and who can ever forget the incredible unforgettable aroma of animals and straw in the exhibition tents?

We all enjoy an opportunity to celebrate. In 1953, in Brunswick Street, that opportunity was provided by the coronation of Queen Elizabeth II, the Union Jacks clearly in evidence. For once dancing in the streets was a reality not simply a figure of speech as can be seen here; though there does seem to be a distinct shortage of menfolk willing to take up the challenge. The couple in the centre of the picture are Henry and Violet Ward who are perhaps hoping to inspire their neighbours to join in. But what is providing the music? There were no 'ghetto blasters' back then to provide the entertainment; what we have is something that was old, even in the 1950s, a barrel organ.

The barrel organ belongs to none other than George and Maud Fawbert, local legends, who are standing in front of their contraption wearing what looks like their pyjamas for the occasion.

Geordie died in 1960 at the age of 86 having, in his lifetime, acquired the status of likeable rogue being well known to the local council, the police and the courts for his habit of bending the rules when it suited him. Geordie and Maud lived in Parkgate for most of their lives and ran many moneymaking enterprises such as fish mongers, coal merchanting and being caravan park owners. Geordie also once ran a bus service in Darlington as well as opening the town's first cycle repair shop.

Above: Anyone who recognises this happy family must be getting a bit long in the tooth now. They are the Lyon Family. 'Who?' younger readers may ask. Older readers will remember 'Life With The Lyons'. Nothing to do with David Attenborough but television's first soap opera. This photograph from the 1950s records a visit by the fictional family to Darlington.

'Life with the Lyons' did not enjoy quite the longevity of Coronation Street or Eastenders but, for a while, it was a hit. But back then it wasn't difficult to be a hit, there were only two channels to watch and even they didn't stay on the air very long.

If we wanted to see moving pictures in colour we had to go to the cinema for the experience. Television broadcasts had begun before the second world war but it was not until the televising of the coronation of Queen Elizabeth II in 1953 that the number of viewers began to soar. The number of television sets began to increase dramatically as prices fell to within the reach of the working man who could rent a set for seven and six a week, falling to five shillings if you kept it for a couple of years. But they were awfully slow to warm up. 'Is it actually switched on?' Would be a regular question as we waited interminably for a picture to appear - and someone would always end up looking behind the set to see if the valves were beginning to glow.

Where has all the water gone? The Baths Hall was a regular venue for exhibitions of various kinds back in the days when Mr Witty was the Baths manager. Built almost to standard design, swimming baths all across the country were boarded over for the winter to allow the premises to be used for other purposes and Darlington's baths were no different. Here is a photo of one such event taken in the 1950s. The stalls are taken by a whole variety of exhibitors many of which will bring back memories of those years. Can you see the Darlington Civil Defence Division's stand for example, a prime example of wartime needs continuing indefinitely into the future as people felt a continuing urge to serve the community long after hostilities had ceased. And there are commercial concerns anxious to

be a visible part of the Darlington scene Burtree Caravans, Hackett and Baines Mattress Repairs and the Brooke Bond Tea stand where visitors are being offered free cup of tea. And what we wonder happened to Easiwork Limited whose stand tells us that their miraculous product cooks a complete family meal in 15 minutes and is guaranteed to half your gas bills as well as improve our health? Things must have been much more advanced then than they are today!

But perhaps the most intriguing feature of the photograph is the thing we can't see. Who on earth was the Amazing Magnetic Man? The sign on the far wall directs us past the bar towards this astonishing individual. Who was he, what did he do and just how amazing was he? We don't know but perhaps some reader with a long memory will write and tell us.

Below: Keep well back please. There may be a large crowd but it doesn't need more than one British bobby to keep things in hand. This police sergeant with his best uniform, white gloves and medals needs no more than a few words and a gentle gesture to keep the crowd in High Row under control on the 27 October 1952. Queen Elizabeth II, who had ascended the throne just eight months earlier, had just taken the salute from the men and officers of the 50th Northumbrian Infantry Division Signals Regiment before unveiling a bookcase in St Cuthbert's Church, built as a memorial to the men who had died for their country in the second world war. Throughout the day the Queen would wear the uniform of the Colonel in Chief of the Royal Signals.

Seldom can a monarch have been more popular. The public had been saddened by the premature death of the Queen's father, George VI, on 6th February 1952 but had been heartened by a new head of state who was both young and beautiful. Somehow the youthful Queen with her handsome husband and growing family embodied optimism and faith in the future against a past which had been so tarnished by economic recession and war.

Here we are in 1953 at a children's Christmas Party held at Pease's Mill. What a year it had been, not least with the coronation of Queen Elizabeth II, following the death of her father the previous year. The nation was understandably obsessed by its new young monarch and on the wall to the left of the Christmas tree is a photograph of Her Majesty dressed in a in a ball gown, one of thousands stuck on walls and homes across the land. Other events of the time however gave less cause for joy. To the right of the Queen is a notice about the National Service Act, a relic of wartime and Empire, which would see thousands upon thousands of our young men whisked off to serve a brief period of their lives in the armed forces. 'And it did me the world of good' has been the oft repeated cry ever since. Almost everyone who did their stint of national service seems to think that today's ill disciplined youngsters would learn a thing or too from a bit of square bashing and having a Sergeant Major shouting 'You 'orrible little man' at them; who knows perhaps it would make people a little better mannered than they seem to be today. Whatever the pros and cons however few of those boys pictured here would ever don a uniform and serve in the Queen's forces. Another indicator of the times is the notice to the left of the Queen about chest x-rays. Who recalls the regular round of visits by the mobile chest x-ray screening van? The x-rays were used to detect TB of the lungs. The incidence of tuberculosis amongst the general population until the 1940s was astonishing with up to a third of the population of Europe being touched by this dread disease. The war against diseases like TB, diphtheria and smallpox was being fought hard with the introduction of new and powerful drugs and backed by the appearance of the National Health Service back in 1948.

At leisure

Above: Paddling pools may be intended for children but in this picture even a couple of mothers have decided to get their feet wet too. Water is irresistible on a hot day and every child used to enjoy going to the local paddling pool until leaks and safety concerns led to their being drained. This paddling pool is an unusual one not being part of a large park or recreation ground. The pool was constructed in Drury Street close to rows of ordinary terraced houses to allow local children the undiluted luxury of taking their shoes and socks off and wading into the water.

These children pictured here in what is probably the early 1950s will have been told not to get their clothes wet and the girls to tuck their skirts into their knickers. They may have been told not to get wet but we can be sure that some did so anyway. Naughty boys inevitably splashed the water with their hands or kicked up waves making the girls shriek and scream with mock terror. And there would always be the more adventurous boy who would try and run through the water and end up falling in. How may children ended up being soaked to the skin and have to make their premature way home in sopping clothes to be dried out by a scolding mother.

Here we are in the early 1950s. The venue is the Baths Hall and the event a formal dinner dance. The pool has been covered over and the hall decorated with bunting, hanging from the ceiling, turning the familiar swimming baths into a perfect venue for entertainment. And what entertainment that was. How people loved to dress up for special occasions; look closely at the dress of the men and women. Men in their dinner jackets, every last one of them in black, forming a sharp contrast to the lovely ladies accompanying them with their evening gowns and fur stoles. How times have changed, these were still the days when arriving at an event in a mink coat resulted in admiring words not thrown eggs and mutters about animal rights.

The event pictured is the annual Territorial Army Dance and a glance up at the makeshift bandstand in the distance reveals a military band all ready to play the kind of music that the diners were all too eager to dance to. The diners of course have yet to finish their meal, the waitresses still taking orders but once the meal has settled and after a comforting cigarette the dancing would begin. And what dances they were not of the head banging shapeless shaking, which would characterise later decades but formal dance such as the foxtrot and the waltz. Ah the waltz, who amongst our readers remembers the last waltz and that chance to walk home through the frosty streets with the object of ones affections in the dark.

The show was a performance by Mr Willie Smith. We don't know what the performance was, but the time is the 1950s, the venue is Pease's mill and we know that a Mr Smith was the factory manager. Perhaps some of those in the audience that day will remember the occasion and let us know. But we don't really need to know what the entertainment was; for us it is the audience which sends us back over five decades, back to a different era, an era before the age of plastic stacking chairs, when hard wood seats with turned wooden legs were what we were expected to sit upon on such occasions. It was also a time when casual dress didn't mean shorts and trainers but a tweed jacket and a slightly less conservative tie than was proper for business hours. But there are always a few rebels, young men who want to be different and flout convention. We can spot at least three of these reckless creatures who have discarded their ties with the same attitude of liberation, which would inspire feminists to burn their bras (or brassieres as we stilled called them) 20 years later. Though if anyone had suggested burning bras back in the 1950s there would have been riots in the streets. Back then going to the cinema to see James Dean in Rebel without a Cause was daring enough. Who could have imagined or predicted the astonishing changes which would take place in the next decade?

Below: It's 1937, two years before the outbreak of the second world war, and here we have the old Theatre Royal captured in film one wet afternoon.

The Theatre Royal was not the first on this site; the original Theatre Royal had been built in 1865 but was destroyed by fire in 1883. When the then new theatre was completed in 1887 it was one of the most up to date provincial theatres in the country featuring tip up chairs and electric lighting. This photograph was taken immediately after the theatre close its doors for the last time. Sadly the Theatre Royal with its red plush seats, gilt carving and scrollwork on the circle and boxes is no more. Following demolition the site was bought by ABC cinemas, which built a new cinema there at the cost of some £50,000. Darlington's Mayor, councillor JH Taylor, opened the cinema in January 1938.

The new 1,600 seat cinema was called the Regal in a coincidental nod towards the old theatre's name and helped provide the town of Darlington with more cinema seats per head of population than any other town in Britain. How many readers today recall visiting the Regal during the years following its opening? Little could anyone have guessed just what appalling scenes of battle, carnage and terror would appear on the silver screen during the years 1939 to 1946 as Mr Chamberlain's famous assurance of 'peace in our time' would prove not to be worth the famous piece of paper it had been written on.

What happened to all these young men and women we wonder? The year is 1936 and this team photograph shows the prizewinners of the gymkhana sports at Pease's Mill.
It's summer, though not quite as warm as we would like, some of the girls are sporting short sleeves others still have their coats on a testament to the variable and unpredictable weather we know all too well. And not just the weather was unpredictable despite the smiles these were the hungry thirties with unemployment a scourge which hit the whole western world and the North East with particular severity. Only the outbreak of the second world war three years later would break the economic logjam and get the economy moving again and bring in full employment for the first time since the early 1920s. The girls in the photograph were unlikely to be thinking about war however on this bright day, although perhaps the men

pictured, obviously older than the girls, may have been thinking about the civil war in Spain. This was the first war since the Russian revolution in which the forces of socialism fought those of capitalism led by General Franco and his fascists. That would be a war of ideologies and many men from the region would leave to join the International Brigade inspired by adventure and their idealistic beliefs in the possibility of a new world order of freedom and equality.

What became of this enchanting group? In the coming years they would face the hardships of war on a scale never before experienced and yet almost all would survive unscathed to marry, start families and grow to adulthood knowing that their adult lives would be infinitely better than their parents, even if the innocent joy of their own childhoods could never be quite the same for their children.

What is going on here? Just look at those legs, not a pair of jeans in sight. Clothing trends change almost imperceptibly, there may be no jeans and trainers but already the fashion for invariably wearing a hat has begun to disappear. The scene is South Park in the mid 1960s, a time when push-chairs were still push-chairs and the deckchair inspired baby buggy had yet to make an appearance. It was a time too when it didn't matter in the least when a pram was too large to fit into the family car since very few of us ordinary folk could afford to buy our own vehicles. We couldn't just pile into a car and take a daytrip to some distant resort but tended to stick to more local venues for our outings.

And South Park was exactly the kind of venue we had in mind. The 100 acre park was given to the town as long ago as 1636 and became the Bellasisi Park in 1853. Sports facilities, the lake and bandstand were provided in 1880 whilst in 1924 a new entrance was added and the site extended in 1930. Who now recalls the boating lake near the old Blackwell corn mill long since silted up and landscaped. Quite what this crowd is gathering to watch is unknown but it must be something good. Maybe one of those youngsters being held high on mum or dad's shoulders remembers the day as one of those magical unforgettable moments from their childhood; happy days indeed.

Do you remember roller skating? It wasn't with those expensive roller boots youngsters today get kitted out with, their wheels in line and fitted with brakes. No, our skates had four wheels, one on each corner as nature intended and had to be strapped onto our shoes. How many twisted ankles and bruised bottoms did we endure? But did we care? Of course not we were going to enjoy ourselves no matter what the cost in bruised bodies and worse, bruised pride, as young men attempted to impress young ladies with their expertise only to discover that their skills on roller skates would never match those of the ice skaters we tried to emulate.

Here in the early 1960s is a photograph of the South Park roller-skating rink with a number of brave souls showing off or attempting to acquire enough skill to attempt a pirouette. Most however found they were content enough if they could just get round once without falling over. Many of the roller skaters are making a decent attempt at the skill, whilst others stand or sit with studied nonchalance at the fence, no doubt trying to look as if they could do anything if they wanted but simply can't be bothered at the moment. How many of those who begged and pestered their parents for a pair of roller skates for Christmas would end up wishing they had never seen the blessed things after being deposited ignominiously on the hard floor for the umpteenth time? And how many parents wished they'd had the foresight to buy a large jar of Germoline after they had come out of the toyshop?

Bird's eye view

Here is a rare view of Darlington's library and art gallery taken by some enterprising cameraman from atop a mill chimney and, judging by the cars parked in Crown Street, pictured during the 1940s. The Renaissance style building was designed by the well-known local architect GG Hoskins who had used red brick from Grosmont near Whitby, red stone from quarries at Dufton, Westmoreland and also stone from the Newbiggin quarry near Carlisle. Edward Pease left £10,000 in his will towards the cost of building the library and those who pass along Crown Street and look upwards will still see the inscription 'Ed. Pease Free Library 1884'. Over the porch of what is now the art gallery are the borough arms with the motto 'Floreat Industria' and the arms of the Pease family with its motto 'Pax et Spes'. The keystone of the arch features the head of Minerva the goddess of learning whilst above her is an owl, the symbol of wisdom, with an open book in its talons.

At the time of its opening the library was heavily dependent upon public donations to fill its shelves. The Mechanics Institute contributed its own 2,500 volumes and another 3,500 books were acquired from the Darlington Subscription Library whilst other gifts and purchases soon enabled the library to offer an impressive number of titles.

Do you look back to your childhood days, borrowing books such as Just William, Biggles and Billy Bunter or reading the many volumes written by Enid Blyton or Arthur Ransome?

Let's hope that the cameraman who took this shot in the 1950s was well wrapped up! The scene is like a Dickens Christmas card. Indeed the times could almost be Victorian, most of the buildings in view dating from that reign.

But of course the photograph is much later than that; if the fact that the picture is obviously taken from an aircraft did not give the game away, then the cars parked in the Market Place would tell us that the date is much later. In fact this delightful winterscape was pictured in the 1950s. The focal point in this, as in so many other pictures of Darlington, is the Town Clock and Covered Market whilst in the distance Bondgate and Woodland Road thread their way westward out of the town.

The almost compete absence of vehicles makes us yearn for the days before traffic was bumper to bumper on every road, though no doubt had the weather not been so bad many more cars would have been about.

A photograph taken today from the same angle would show many changes: the buildings on the lower right hand corner have gone, replaced by the Cornmill Centre; those in the lower left corner by the Dolphin Centre and the block of buildings formed by the junction of Bondgate and Northgate being redeveloped as part of the Queen Street Centre. Despite the proliferation of 'centres' Darlington, unlike many towns, has fortunately been able to preserve much of the best of its Victorian architecture.

The centre of Darlington has changed a great deal since this bird's eye view was taken. Some things may have remained unaltered, St Cuthbert's church remains but the shopping centre has been altered dramatically with a great swathe of buildings in the bottom centre of the scene having gone to make way for the modern Cornmill Centre. At the heart of this aerial photograph, indeed at the heart of Darlington itself, is the Town Clock and Covered Market both built in 1864 and designed by that well-known architect Alfred Waterhouse. The buildings were ready just in time for the creation of Darlington as an independent Municipal Borough in 1867. Since its construction the clock tower, built in the Italianate style, has become a symbol of Darlington. Below the covered market, with its scattering of parked cars, can be clearly seen the Open Market; to the left of the Open Market can be seen the Nissen hut businesses where food was sold at remarkably reasonable prices.

To the left of Nissen huts was the old Leadyard bus station serving the villages and towns surrounding Darlington; the bus station is now long gone having disappeared beneath the new Town Hall.

To the top of the frame can be seen the roof of the United bus depot. The United site would eventually become the Safeway Supermarket. Another Alfred Waterhouse building to the right of the Town Clock is Barclays Bank on High Row, originally Bankhouses Bank, and rebuilt in 1864.

On the move

J oseph Pease gazes down from his plinth looking south along Prebend row to a scene which has changed dramatically since this photograph was taken in the late 1940s. The traffic, in those days before the by-pass, is nose to tail and the lady on the far right standing below the railings separating Prebend Row from High Row is apprehensively holding her hand to her mouth; no doubt she is wondering just exactly how long it will be before a gap in the traffic will give her the chance to cross.

There are an immense number of features of obvious interest here and a magnifying glass will reveal many more. Most prominent amongst the changes however is the absence today of trolley busses whose power lines crisscross this picture.

The ornate lamp stands seen here would be replaced by more effective but far less attractive replacements in the late 1950s, whilst later still, the facade of the buildings would change significantly with the arrival of the Cornmill shopping centre.

And are you old enough to remember cobbled streets? Though much of the road surface here has already been covered with tarmacadam the lady mentioned earlier is stood on a section of road which is still covered with cobble stones, a common feature then when many horses were still around and the town planners wisely left gradients cobbled to allow horse shoes a better grip, not to mention the far less efficient car tyres of the day.

F eetham's field was once a real field where
sheep and cattle grazed but it was used for
many other purposes over the years. There is
little sign of any grass growing in the early
1950s in this view taken looking east over the invisible
River Skerne; in fact the river passes in front of the
buildings seen behind these parked vehicles.

What a fascinating collection of cars and vans this is.
And not just cars and lorries: at the very rear are a
couple of ancient caravans, the forerunners of modern
mobile homes, with their chimneys poking out of their
roofs reminding us that, back then, even caravans used
coal for heating.
One glance at these cars instantly takes us back to the

days before seat belts were compulsory, when petrol was priced in shillings per gallon not pence per litre and when 40 miles an hour was good going over streets which were often cobbled or only tarmacced down the middle of the road. None of these vehicles would ever tear down a motorway at 90 miles an hour! Unusually this photograph makes it easy to identify the car number plates or 'motor-car index marks' as they were officially called. Were you a car spotter in your youth? If so you should be able to tell where these cars came from: BBT 69 on the left was from Newcastle-upon-Tyne and VN 4590 from the North Riding whilst AAJ 258 is a real foreigner having come from far away Southampton.

Above: What a riveting scene here in Northgate. And what a wealth of detail. Get your magnifying glass out if you wish and pour over this people packed picture of yesteryear. And it is so often in the minutiae that one finds ones memories being pricked; when did that road side sign which reads 'Motor Bus Stop' disappear and where is that lorry with the earth moving equipment on it heading for?

No date is available for this photo, even though the clock in the middle distance tells us it is twenty five minutes past eleven and the throng of shoppers suggests the day is a Saturday. But judging the vehicles and fashions it would appear to have been taken sometime in the 1960s, at a time when the Ford Anglia had made its appearance and just before hemlines began to edge above the knee.

The sight of a coach reminds us that Northgate was once part of the Great North Road stretching from Edinburgh to London. What a bottleneck Darlington could be in those days and on some occasions those sat fuming in traffic jams could be forgiven for the hope that one day the town could be wiped off the map.

Fortunately for us the town was not obliterated to make way for cars. The queues of traffic were relieved in 1965 by the building of the Darlington bypass built along the line of the old Merrybent railway.

What year was this photograph taken? The record says it was 14th August but we must guess at the year, which judging by the two cars parked on the left, is in the late 1950s or early 1960s. The scene however is Bondgate, on the No 1 bus route with the bus in view headed for Bishop Auckland via Shildon and Heighington. On the left, by the nearest parked car, is a chemist's shop with its weighing scales outside the door. Put a penny in the slot and you'd normally get an accurate, if unwelcome, reminder of how much one weighed - though this particular set of scales looks to be parked on a slope which might affect its accuracy. How many times though have we watched enormous women struggle out of their coats and remove their shoes trying to shed every spare ounce of extra weight before getting on the scales to receive the bad news? Darlington has a history of flooding going back centuries. The flood of 1753 is one often referred to in the history books when the Tees rose above the high water mark by an astonishing 15ft not only washing away the turnpike house and the £50 in toll money which it contained but caused untold damage elsewhere. The Great Flood however came in November 1771 when coffins were swept out of their graves and the whole town was reduced to looking like Venice.

If the doom-mongers are right and global warming occurs Darlington may be looking at repeating this experience in the 21st century.

Below: 'Move down the bus please'. 'Ay thank yew'. Arthur Askey didn't need anyone to explain what he was talking about when he coined these catch phrases. We all used buses then. Some youngsters today are so used to being ferried everywhere by car that they wouldn't know a bus ticket from a lottery ticket. These were still the days when more people travelled to work by bus than by private transport, and the buses in the foreground, each labelled 'Duplicate', are evidence of the necessity to put on extra buses at peak times. But what was so special about the 14th January 1963?

That's the date this photo was taken of the old bus station.

Trolley buses had finally disappeared into history just six years before this photograph was taken, although the town had actually used its first petrol driven buses as far back as 1927 when four buses had been hired. The trouble with those first motor buses was that they were extremely uncomfortable to ride in and the council received a barrage of complaints from passengers. Trolley buses and trams with their electric motors and few moving parts provided an

immeasurably smoother ride than the early internal combustion engines. Darlington's buses were originally liveried in deep blue until the later council decreed a change to cream. The diesel buses which replaced the trolley buses were faster and more versatile than their electric rivals, not to mention more economical to run since they required no overhead cables which needed to maintained.

Bottom right: Snow. And plenty of it. This is the winter of 1961 in a photograph taken looking southwards along Prebend Row from Prospect Place. At work employees are looking out of the windows of the factories and shops hoping the snow will stop and not make it difficult for them to get home after they have finished their day. At school children are praying that the snow will come down even harder; with luck they will be sent home early and have chance to get out their sledges and toboggans. Well nothing pleases everybody as the saying goes.

It's exactly ten o'clock in the morning and everyone in view is wishing they were somewhere else, not least the passenger of the van in the foreground who by the looks of it is having to help push the vehicle along through the slush. In fact the road surface doesn't look too bad, certainly not as bad as it would be the following year, nor half so bad as it was in 1947 - but then these were the days before minimum tread depths were required on motor vehicles, so maybe the driver wasn't getting quite as much traction as one might expect. In many respects this scene remains unaltered; the Clock Tower is still there and, despite road improvements over the years, High Row and Prebend Row are still there too. What has changed however are the buildings on the left of the picture, with significant changes made to accommodate the creation of the Cornmill shopping centre.

What a wonderful sight for nostalgia addicts. A row of Darlington trolley buses lined up for this photograph taken in the 1940s.

Darlington's love affair with powered public transport began in 1862 with the early introduction of steam trams run by the Darlington Street Railroad Company. By 1865 however the firm had run into financial difficulties and in a strange backward step the steam trams were replaced by horse drawn vehicles.

It was not until 1902 that the council decided the time was ripe for electrification when it bought up the horse tram network for the sum of £7,000; the last horse drawn tram ran in August 1903. Five miles of electrified track were then laid that met at Prebend Row. Some sixteen single-decker electric trams were bought with open cabs. The new system opened on 1st June 1904. The first trolley buses appeared on Darlington's streets in 1928 running from outside the Midland Bank in Northgate and travelling to West Auckland Road. By the following year, when pneumatic tyres were introduced, the council had a fleet of 48 Straker-Clough, Ransome, English Electric and Leyland trolley buses in its fleet. Sadly trolley buses were phased out during the 1950s with the last journey being made in 1957. By June 1958 the whole system had disappeared, the overhead cables becoming nothing but a fond memory for older residents who, if they shut their eyes, can still recall the electric whine the trolley bus engines made as they set off.

Above: Doesn't the name The Great North Road sound so much better than the A1? This photo of the junction at Harrowgate Hill taken around 1960 shows that the road was busy enough to warrant a traffic policeman to be on duty to keep traffic flowing smoothly on this main artery.

Just under the policeman's white gloved arm can be seen a mini, the first of a new generation of cars with their front wheel drive and transverse engines which would soon sweep away the all black bone shakers with their running boards and stick out indicators which are so prominent in this scene.

Just to the right of the North End Post office is a boy on his bicycle waiting for the policemen's permission to cross the road. For most of us bicycles were still heavy, sturdy beasts, with good broad leather saddles and rod brakes were still the norm though gradually being replaced by the much lighter cable brakes.

In the far distance, rounding the corner and coming past the White Horse hotel, is a Leyland bus, one of a fleet, which had monopolised Darlington's public transport for less than three years. These were the days when bus conductors and conductresses were the norm and as a consequence buses ran faster than they do today since the driver did not have to wait to collect fares before setting off. One man-operated buses may be cheaper to run but they certainly aren't more efficient for the unhappy passenger. And now you can't even have a cigarette on the top deck to help pass the time either!

Shopping spree

Taken around 1960 this photograph features two shops in Horsemarket. On the left is the WH Smith & Son Old English Tea Rooms, complete with a pub-like sign hanging from the wall, perhaps giving those who would prefer a pot of ale to a pot of tea some psychological comfort. Booksellers and newsagents the WH Smith organisation traces its origins, most appropriately here in Darlington, to the earliest days of the railways when the original WH Smith set up business providing railway passengers with reading material.

To the right of WH Smith's is J Lear & Sons' ironmongery and hardware store. The shop proudly announces that it was established as long ago as 1760 and no doubt at the time this picture was taken its owners imagined that it might go on for as long again. In fact Lear & Sons would very soon cease operating from this site. In front of Lears is a cyclist who is staring curiously at the camera; a point worth making about the bicycle is the white paint on the rear mudguard, an important feature for night visibility and a carry over from the war years and the blackout. Something else is very white in the picture too: the traffic policeman's gloves. Working on point duty was part of every policeman's lot. Although traffic lights, to control the flow of traffic, had appeared decades earlier their introduction was a slow process and so the sight of a policeman directing traffic at busy intersections was still a familiar one in every town until the late 1960s.

Half a century ago, in August 1951, when this photograph was taken High Row looked very much as it does today.
But it had not always look like this. Exactly 50 years earlier High Row was subject to major reconstruction; before then, instead of being built on two different levels, the upper part of High Row was simply a cobbled incline that sloped gently down to join Prebend Row making one very wide road. On busy market days the whole slope would be filled with horses, carts and tradesmen all eager to sell their wares. It was only in 1901 that this ancient arrangement came to an end and today's terrace was constructed along with steps and iron railings for the safety of pedestrians. Behind High Row once stretched former medieval burgage plots ending in back lanes such as Skinnergate and connected to High Row by Post House Wynd, the narrow lane which takes its name from having once being the location of a posting house, the Talbot Inn. Before the advent of the post the Wynd had been called Glover's Wynd. Although High Row may be unaltered in many respects in other ways it has changed significantly since this scene was captured, not least by the relative reduction in cars, as traffic has been systematically diverted away from the town centre. As for shops, the scene has changed too; here Binns, the Home and Colonial, the cleaners and chemists, and John Grisdale are all in view reminding us of days long gone.

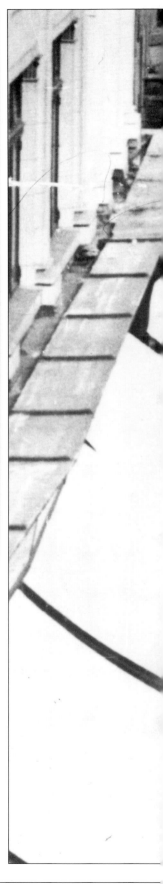

Below: The flags are flying outside the Hole in the Wall public house to celebrate Whit Monday in 1955. Remarkably for a Bank Holiday the day is a hot one, and those who are milling around here in the Market Place walking between the stalls are no doubt working up a thirst which will be satisfied in the Hole in the Wall. Certainly the stallholders are getting hot, one of whom has taken off his jacket and thrown it onto the canvas top of his stall out of the way. In recent times the Market Place has been extensively refurbished with new cobblestones, seating and other permanent decorations.

Still just within living memory the Spring Fair was a hiring fair where labourers would come to offer their services to farmers for the coming season.

Beyond the market is the spire of St Cuthbert's church which was built between the years 1183 and 1230, though the belfry, spire and aisles are 14th century. As a collegiate church it had prebends - canons supported by rent from local properties and later a dean. The unusual name Prebend Row for Darlington's main street takes its name from those clerical posts.

The church is often referred to as 'The Lady of the North' whose slender lancet windows and steep roofs enhance its beauty. Indoors the church is laid out to a traditional cruciform plan with a processional west door.

What would the church's founder, Bishop Pudsey, have made of us no longer holidaying at Whitsuntide?

High Row was originally called the Headrow. Much of High Row and Skinnergate was destroyed on May 7th 1589 when fire broke out in the old town and destroyed almost 300 houses. Along with Skinnergate High Row is one of the oldest roads in Darlington and has been virtually rebuilt more than once over the centuries.

This early photograph was in all probability taken from Binns' department store on the corner of High Row. One of the Binns' delivery vans is prominently parked in the foreground.

Exactly when this photo was taken is a matter of some debate. We can guess that it was a market day from the thronging crowd, the sheer number of parked cars and the outspread awnings; but what year was it?

The records indicate that the year was 1930 but the Belisha beacon in the centre of the scene, and only introduced in 1935, clearly demonstrates that a later date than that previously attributed to it is the correct one. Judging by the fashions and vehicles we would guess that in fact this picture was taken not much before the outbreak of the second world war. High Row would not see the footpath as full of pedestrians nor the road as full of cars for some years to come: young men would become conspicuous by their absence and those that were in evidence would bewaring military uniforms, not flat caps and trilbies, whilst car headlights would be cowled and petrol rationed for the next few years putting many cars in their garages for the duration of the war.

It's a summer's afternoon in the early 1960s in Post House Wynd. People are strolling past Ideal Fisheries the fish and chip shop, that staple diet of those turning out from the pubs at closing times - and no competition yet from Chinese takeaways or Curry houses. Across the road, on the right, is Winterschladen's, wine and a spirit merchant. Opposite Winterschladen's is E & L Cleugh, newsagents with its multiple adverts for cigarettes. This photograph was taken just around the time that smokers got the bad news that tobacco might be doing them more harm than good. It would take a few years for the message to sink in however, and some of the best adverts on the television were for cigarettes; who can ever forget phrases like 'Cool as a mountain stream' and 'You're never alone with a Strand'. Curiously, although being regarded as technically one of the best adverts ever made, sales of Strand cigarettes never took off; television viewers associated themselves with the man in the advert's disappointment at being let down by his date rather than the subsequent comfort he got from lighting up.

Here we are in Northgate some 30 years ago. Northgate was once the location of Darlington's ducking stool where nagging wives could be taken to have some of the shrew taken out of them: goodness knows what today's feminist and women's rights agitators would make of it if anyone proposed reintroducing that old custom!

The old properties in Northgate were largely cleared away to make room for the inner ring road. This scene however will bring back memories for those readers who once strolled along the shops lining the road when it was still part of the A1, the Great North Road. Did you used to go shopping for clothes at Paige's, we can just see the carefully packed glassware, still being delivered in tea chests to Altham's, next door, when this photo was taken. Or did you browse through the racks at Wilsons' Fashion Centre? Or maybe the Surplus Goods store next to Wilsons was more your type of shop with its promise of 'top quality goods at lowest prices'.

If shopping wasn't to your taste did you once sink a cheerful pint of Cameron's at the Bay Horse at the corner of Albion Street? And of course Northgate was not just noted for its shops but was also a centre of entertainment. What about the Assembly Hall which became the Astoria? Dear old Jack Warner of Dixon of Dock Green fame performed there, as did Molly Sugden later famed as Mrs Slocombe in Are You Being Served? before it became a bingo club. Whilst also found in Northgate was the Regal cinema seating 1,600 patrons.

Above: It's the late 1950s in Blackwellgate and one of the last times trolley bus cables were to be seen. The time is ten to four and all is well with the world or it seems so but in fact this would be one of the last chances to photograph Blackwellgate with it trolley bus cables hanging over the roadway. The sight of those cables shout out to us of a now almost forgotten age. The first of Darlington's trolleybuses made its inaugural journey in March 1925. A premature decision to scrap the trolleybuses was made in 1946 and replace them with buses. The last time a trolley bus ran in Darlington however was in July 1957; the whole network was finally demolished by June of the following year. It's strange now looking back and recalling that the trolleybuses were once state of the art transport replacing the electric trams which had themselves replaced horse drawn trams in 1903.

But trolley buses apart what of the rest of this sunny scene? In the distance can be a number of cars, almost invariably black in honour of Henry Ford who said you can have them in any colour you like - as long as its black. And if you were fortunate enough to have a car there was no difficulty in parking, unlike today when the idea of simply pulling up outside a shop is as much a part of the history books as the Magna Carta.

But even If we'd known of the pollution and congestion, which would come in our lifetimes, would we have opted to keep things as they were? Probably not, we love our cars too much.

S pot the difference. This almost identical view of Blackwellgate was taken in the early 1960s. At first the differences are not too obvious, there are still exactly the same number of chimney pots. Bainbridge Barker, the Harrods of Darlington, is still there on the left and the pepper pots still visible in the far distance, as they would continue to be until 1978. Even the clock tells the same time ten to four. The most obvious difference of course is that those trolley bus cables have now gone but spotting all the other differences requires closer inspection.

The ornate cast iron street lights have been replaced by concrete, whilst traffic lights along with keep left signs along the pedestrian refuge have made their appearance, testimony to the increase in road traffic in just a few short years. Perhaps one of the most difficult changes to spot is that which has occurred to the facade of the Falchion pub whose Dutch gable in the earlier photograph has been removed and replaced by a tiled roof.

The Falchion was once known as the Three Blue Bells and until 1984 was noted for the 8 foot long sword or Falchion which it used as a sign. The pub took its name from the type of sword used by a knight with the name of Conyers who slew the great Sockburn worm, or dragon, in the 13th century. Conyers killed the beast with the falchion and was given the manor of Sockburn.

We tend to think of exotic cuisine in the form of Indian and Chinese restaurants as a phenomenon of the 1970s and 80s but here is proof to the contrary. In this 1960s photograph of Northgate, Darlington, can be seen the Ying Hung Chinese restaurant above Peter's and to the right of the British Home Stores, later BHS.

No one then had heard of MacDonald's or Pizza palaces - but they would come, we only had to wait.

In the distance can be seen the Burtons building next door to Marks and Spencer's. Once 'Marks and Sparks' was the shop to buy ones clothes in but, like Burtons before it, it would eventually suffer from adverse market forces and changes in the public's taste for fashion which would leave

the company in serious difficulties for some years. And what about that Army Information Office, above Alexandre's? We still needed an awful lot of soldiers when this photo was taken. True, much of the Empire had disappeared, India, the Jewel in the Crown, had become independent as far back as 1948 but there were still many outposts left to defend, Hong Kong, Aden and Cyprus not to mention those parts of Africa such as Rhodesia where Ian Smith and his white settlers had yet to declare UDI - their unilateral declaration of independence in the face of the British governments intention to hand over the country to its indigenous population. UDI worked for a while but the winds of change referred to by Harold Macmillan were unstoppable.

At work

On a sunny summers day during the second world war a photographer has captured the many women drivers and two men of the driving pool of the Aycliffe Ordnance Factory, pictured in front of their collection of vehicles.

The war years would see hundreds of thousands of women in various uniforms for the first time serving in a whole range of roles which could no longer been done by men who had been called up to serve in the army, navy and airforce.

Many of the woman working on the home front worked in ordnance factories, or engineering establishments making vital equipment and munitions for the war effort. During the war many existing factories switched production to the war effort producing bullets, bombs, detonators, shells and explosives. The Aycliffe Industrial Estate would eventually be built on the site of the ordnance factory.

Whilst those who helped on the land were dubbed land girls and were almost invariably young the Aycliffe driving pool, seems to be a mixed group with a quite large age range. Perhaps its not surprising the number of women who could drive at the beginning of the war was very small with those who could tending to be old enough to have husbands who could afford to own a car and teach them. Even long after the war it was still a rare sight to see a woman driving a car and it would not be until the 1970s that as many woman as men were taking their driving tests.

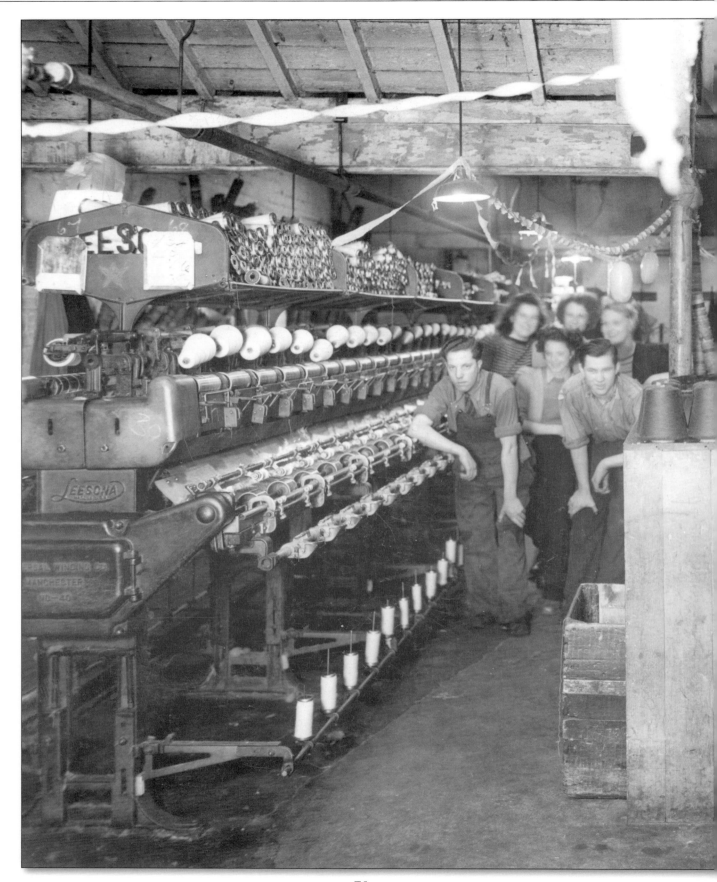

With the exception of George Stephenson no name is more familiar to the residents of Darlington than that of the Pease family. It's Christmas-time in the 1950s and here we are in the winding department at Pease's mill. The factory would provide an income for thousands and ensure that Christmas presents and a turkey would be available in homes throughout the town.

These four young men and dozen women are posing for the camera beside the machinery which they toiled over day after day but it was not all work and no play and the fact that it is the festive season is well evidenced by the paper decorations hanging from the ceiling.

The Pease family had arrived in Darlington in the middle of the 18th century and at first worked in woollens and linen before moving into every kind of industry imaginable: railways, banking, coal, stone quarrying, brick making and water works. The family made a vast fortune, though their Quaker background would imbue them with strong philanthropic tendencies.

By 1816 the Pease mill in Darlington was already employing 600 workers and it would be Edward Pease (1779-1842) who would, in 1925, be the main driving force behind establishing the Stockton and Darlington railway earning for himself the title of 'Father of the Railways'. The staff pictured here probably weren't giving much thought to the history of the Pease family: they would possibly be thinking of the dances they may be going to over the holiday period and whether they would meet the boy or girl of their dreams there?

Above: Cor! What a cracker. Whatever happened to the young lady with the film star looks sitting next to the chap in the flat cap? With looks like that she must have been a dead cert to be carnival queen of 1939.

But such frivolity must have been far from people's minds when this picture was taken. This photograph was taken in what must have been the most worrying year of the twentieth century - 1939.

The location is the Houndgate warehouse of Henry Pease & Co and the young women sitting around the table are assembling gas masks.

Everyone in this picture would have known a father, brother or friend who had suffered from being 'gassed' during the Great War which had ended just 21 years earlier, and no-one then doubted that Adolf Hitler might well drop gas bombs on the British Isles.

If Hitler was going to commit such evil the British would be prepared. Everyone was issued with a gas mask, the

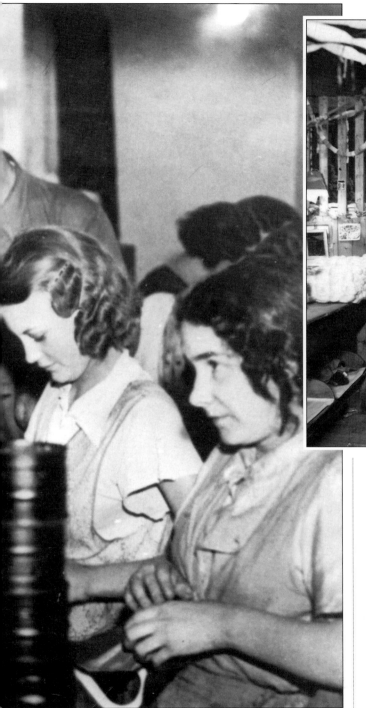

Top: Here we are in the Hanking Room at Pease's mill. It's Christmas in the 1950s and here we see the mill manager Mr Smith seated on one of those ever present wooden chairs, whilst the five ladies in the department form a half circle around him. Who said that in those days a gentleman always gave up his seat for a lady? And whatever happened to those pinafores? There was a time when every self respecting housewife could be seen sporting a wrap around pinny but they seem to have gone the way of the Dodo, though we do hear of a few ladies who still have one about which they wear whilst doing their dusting and cooking.

It's doubtful though that many of the virtually anonymous wives of the Pease family wore such items of clothing; they would have had servants to do their domestic chores for them. And its unlikely that such servants, or at least female domestic staff, would have been permitted to wear trousers to work, as the young lady on the left of this picture appears to be doing. Trousers for women made their first regular appearance amongst the Land Army girls during the second world war but generally a strict dress code was applied in all walks of life. Men wore collars and ties for work and women wore dresses or skirts. It would not be for another thirty years that a woman wearing trousers would become so common as to be unremarkable.

standard variety was carried everywhere in its cardboard box. Millions of the standard gas masks were produced for the public, with variants for children, babies and members of the forces and civil defence. They looked quite scary when put on, although to make them more acceptable to children red and blue, rather than plain black, were introduced for the little ones in the form of Mickey Mouse gas masks. Whole body gas masks, which could be pumped with a bellows, were provided for babies.

Though Darlington may be famed across the world as the birthplace of the railways nevertheless steam locomotion was far from being its only industry. The chemical and insulating company Drachem, for example, which processed the local magnesian limestone or dolomite for industrial insulation and for use in the printing, plastics, synthetic rubber, ceramics, glass and toiletries markets arrived in 1927. In 1947 two other large firms brought employment to the area: Paton and Baldwin's and Alexander's. Both firms particularly offered employment opportunities for women. Paton and Baldwin's made knitting yarns and employed in excess of a thousand workers, whilst another five hundred worked at Alexander's, which manufactured clothing for men.

This scene, capture by the camera in the 1950s, shows four of the girls at Paton and Baldwin's each wearing overalls bearing the distinctive P&B logo on their front pocket.

What's going on? Perhaps the three girls to the rear are being shown how to tie one length of yarn from the end of an empty bobbin to the start of a new one by their supervisor.

One cannot help but wonder what happened to these young women later in their lives; judging by the absence of wedding rings they have yet to sail into the sea of matrimony but, before long, they would be doing so. Today there is every likelihood that they are grandmothers, and perhaps they still meet from time to time and share recollections of their youth.

Sadly Paton and Baldwin's factory would close in the 1960s.

Pease's Mill, the Reeling Department in early 1950s. It's late December and if the Christmas decorations didn't give the time of year away those warm fur-lined boots surely would. Were those Christmas decorations bought from Woolworth's we wonder, or had these ladies done what so many did during the austere years of the 1940s and 50s and made there own? Without the decorations though the long room with its clanking machinery would have looked far less inviting and perhaps even frightening for a youngster starting her first day at work. But the place was not really so bad; there was a camaraderie to be found amongst those who worked there which is rarely found today. Perhaps it was the shared experience of the war years which had made people more considerate of one another or perhaps it was the relative simplicity of life compared with today which often made the workplace somewhere where lifelong friendships were forged, rather than somewhere simply to earn ones living. That idea of a family experience was certainly something which was well applied to Pease's mill, with many being able to say that their parents and grandparents had worked there all their lives.

No wonder that Darlington's most prominent public memorial is of a member of the Pease family - the statue of Joseph Pease (1799-1872) dominating High Row honouring him as the first ever Quaker MP. The statue was unveiled in 1875 to mark the Golden Jubilee of the opening of the Stockton and Darlington Railway.

Building better homes

Home is where the heart is. And a local firm which has put its heart into building homes for a century is Bussey & Armstrong, a company which in its long life has almost certainly been responsible for building more homes in Darlington than any other.

Today Bussey & Armstrong is part of the Darlington based, and locally owned group, that includes Estill Cooper Construction.

The firm's yard and headquarters are in Brinkburn Road, a site, which until 1940, was the home of the Liberal MP for Cleveland Henry Fell Pease. The fine Victorian mansion was named Brinkburn. The lodge for Brinkburn was in Woodland Road; today the entire estate is now covered with modern housing.

But those modern houses were still far in the future when in 1902 Alfred Banting Armstrong and William Bussey, who were both already working in the building trade, decided to form a partnership as house builders and saw millers. Their original premises were in Hopetown from where they began building the first houses in Trafalgar Terrace using imported timber and horse drawn carts.

By 1928 the partnership was sufficiently well established to enable it to buy a 25 acre site at Cockerton, from the Darlington Corporation. They planned to build a new garden suburb of 300 houses ensuring work for 120 employees for the next three years.

The scheme was very popular at the start of the 'hungry thirties' as it also provided additional employment in trades supplying materials. Alfred Armstrong, by now sole proprietor, was proud of using local materials and estimated that the houses would use half a million bricks, all made at the local brickworks. The site was close to the then new chemical factory bounded by Bates Avenue, West Auckland Road, The LNER Barnard Castle branch line and Stooperdale Avenue.

The garden suburb had primarily been devised to provide homes for when the chemical works opened.

Below: *An early solid-tyre tipper-truck used by the company for the delivery of sand and gravel.*

The houses, priced at £400, were thoroughly modern, semi detached, each with three bedrooms, a living room, kitchen and scullery together with a garden. Even for the times they were a bargain and they incorporated 'every modern convenience'.

It is interesting to consider what exactly constituted 'every modern convenience' at those inter-war periods. Mr Armstrong was offering sunk switches in oxy-copper as an impossible to resist feature. An early advertisement for the firm promised that not only would the houses be modern and comfortable but that they would also be 'designed so that every scheme enhances the beauty of the district'.

These days we take owner occupation for granted; for ordinary working class people however that idea is quite modern; most of our recent ancestors rented their homes. A whole section of the firm's sales booklet for the period is devoted to buying houses by ordinary peo- ple, an idea not taken for granted by anyone then. It points out 'after all you do not rent your furniture or your car; so why should you expect someone to loan you a house?' Clear instructions are given on how to apply to a building society for a loan and how the society would expect to be repaid. Over the years hundreds of

This page: *A sample of post war housing built by the company.*

Darlington's population would take advantage of the invitation to buy a home; and what a fabulous investment they would turn out to be; just look at how much those £400 homes cost today!

Bussey & Armstrong wanted to bring to Darlington the garden city atmosphere typified by Welwyn in the south of England. The extent to which they would succeed is evidenced to this day with grass bordered pavements and rows of now mature trees.

But housing was not the whole story. In 1950 the firm temporarily suspended house building to concentrate on the new High School building.

Since 1985 the company has been owned by Estill Cooper construction which carries forward the firm's founding principles. Working with local architects to ensure imaginative designs and layouts and using quality materials and workmanship provided by a directly employed workforce and long standing partnerships with specialist subcontractors, the continuing aim is to provide high quality, well designed yet affordable homes across the market. And the firm remains committed to preserving and creating a quality environment.

The Woodlands Estate would be typical of the style in its walled parkland setting and whatever the price range the company would continue to enjoy a reputation for housing the people of Darlington in homes that could be depended upon for convenience and value for money as well as enhancing the environment. These properties were traditional in design using real Welsh slate, brick and lead glazing. The company employed its own blacksmith to make finials and railings.

At the opening of the new millennium Bussey & Armstrong was able to announce its latest plans for a £60 million investment to transform a 115 acre site on the outskirts of Darlington at Faverdale. The ten year plan would see the creation of a major new community on the Northwest fringes of the town beginning with the former Darchem works.

A major benefit for the town of the 'West Park Project' would be the long overdue transformation of a former industrial eyesore into the first new public park for over 50 years. The company planned to landscape a 30 acre brown field site to create a green heart for both the existing and expanding community to enjoy, which would integrate existing old habitats with newly created recreational space in an environment which would seem more like living in the country, than in the town. The project aimed to create not only a variety of new housing, but also new local amenities including a new NHS community health facility as well as an extensive sports and recreational area.

Home may be where the heart is, but it helps if the builder has a heart as well.

Above: *A Bussey & Armstrong invoice from 1944.*
Below: *New property built in the traditional style on the Tees Grange estate in Darlington.*

Getting along swimmingly

It only seems like yesterday when the site of the Dolphin Public House was transformed into one of the largest leisure centres in the North of England. For the people of Darlington the Dolphin Centre represented many years of planning, designing, lobbying and preparing. The end result of which was a multi-sport leisure centre on three different levels, offering a wide range of social, sporting and recreational activities.

The original Kendrew and Gladstone Street swimming baths located on Gladstone Street in Darlington were demolished two weeks after the opening of the first phase of the Dolphin Centre and a car park now stands on the site. The Centre first opened its doors in 1982 and many expectant and excited swimmers took advantage of the modern state-of-the-art facilities on offer. In the early days the queues to visit the Dolphin Pool Complex would extend out of the temporary entrance, facing the Town Hall and run most of the way along the length of the outside of the building underneath the Dolphin Centre emblems visible in the photograph below.

The official opening was performed in 1982 by Sir Roger Bannister. That was the time when all of the many facilities in the centre became operational, including the sauna and steam room areas, squash courts, five-a-side football pitches, fitness room, table tennis and badminton courts, as well as numerous exercise and coaching courses and much, much more.

The Dolphin Centre's main focal point for many years for young and old were the swimming pools, complete with the high diving boards, training pool, toddler pool and the main twenty-five by eighteen metre swimming pool. Initially the pools complex opened without either of the two exciting slides that we see today but within a few years 'Whoosh' and 'Winder' were designed and installed.

Above: The Sports Council Management Award, won by the Dolphin Centre in 1994.
Below: The Dolphin Centre.

The Dolphin Centre has hosted many large as well as small events during the last twenty years, for example the famous annual holiday fair organised by the Northern Echo. Other events included within the Dolphin Centre's portfolio are fashion shows, concerts, boxing tournaments and events in connection with Children in Need, It's a Knockout, Superstar and Charity workouts. It has also been the venue for Ministerial visits and even Prime Ministerial keynote speeches. The annual Mayor's Ball has been held here since 1982. There have also been taikwondo tournaments, international and national swimming galas, disability swimming galas and a host of other things.

Prior to the opening of the Dolphin Centre in 1982 the Gladstone Street and Kendrew Baths hosted many wrestling events that attracted hundreds of spectators from all over the region to watch TV favourites. These included such famous names as Kendo Nagasaki, Cat-Weasel, Giant Haystacks and Big Daddy to name but a few. These family favourites all moved with the times and hosted many similar events in the Dolphin Centre main sport hall that would house over twelve hundred spectators stamping their feet to the encouragement of the wrestling stars. In more recent times such events have been superseded by the WWF with such big names as The Rock, The Undertaker, Triple H and Stone Cold Steve Austin.

The Dolphin Centre has attracted over 128 million visitors to the facilities over the last twenty years. Visitors have come from as far and wide as America, South Africa, New Zealand, Australia and mainland Europe.

Some things you might not know about the Dolphin Centre:

Did you know that the main pool holds 134,400 gallons of water?

Did you know that the Central Hall of the Dolphin Centre was originally built in the late 18th Century as a Quaker Meeting House? It was then used as a cinema followed by being the site of the old rents and rates hall.

Top: *'Winder,' one of the Swimming Pool slides.*
Above left: *One of the many fashion shows hosted by The Dolphin Centre.*

Did you know that some famous visitors that have been to the Dolphin Centre Central Hall include Charles Dickens, Sir Robert Peel, Benjamin Disraeli and Sir Roger Bannister, not forgetting more recently the Prime Minister, Tony Blair?

Did you know the Dolphin Centre has an average of over one million visitors annually?

The Pulse Suites and fitness room annually have 100,000 visitors, that's over 2,300 per week or 325 visitors per day attempting to stay fit and healthy.

There are around 2,500 children's birthday parties a year held there and some 350,000 swimmers visiting the Dolphin Centre's Pool complex every year.

The Dolphin Centre has achieved much in its relatively short life-span, but one of the highlights was to be chosen to compete in the National Sports Council Management Awards. In 1994 the Dolphin Centre was successful in its application and was awarded the UK National management Award from the Sports Council of the UK. This competition was held to determine who was offering the leading facilities for leisure at the time. There was fierce competition with over three hundred entries from centres throughout the length and breadth of the country and both the Centre's staff and the residents of Darlington were holding their breath as the results were awaited. The Dolphin Centre came out on top, which was an occasion for justified civic pride and great rejoicing among the Centre's staff who work hard to maintain the high standards of the facilities on offer. Although many things have changed since 1994, the Dolphin Centre staff are committed to providing continuous improvement and innovation so that in the present climate of competition the facilities are regularly visited by the people of Darlington.

The extensive sport and fitness programmes offered at the centre are supplemented by an outstanding catering

service, which has recently achieved ISO 9002 accreditation. No order is too small or large for the chefs - from breakfast to afternoon tea in the Cafeteria, to buffet lunches in the Restaurant and luxurious banquets in the Main Hall. Rooms are also available for hire for private functions.

Getting fit and looking good doesn't have to be difficult and can be enjoyable. It has been proven that exercise makes you feel better and look better, helps you cope with stress and generally gives you more energy to make the most out of life. Fitness experts recommend you attend the centre a minimum of three times each week and exercise when possible for one hour, using a mixture of Aerobic and Weights equipment. They are confident you will enjoy your visits to the centre and that you will soon notice an improvement in your body condition, as well as looking and feeling better.

Above left: *The wrestler 'Big Daddy'.*
Below: *A boat display in the main swimming pool.*

Creche facilities are also provided with the aim of allowing busy Mums and Dads to use the Centre's facilities. Children are fully supervised by qualified nursery staff whilst they enjoy two hours of mixed activity with children of a similar age. Limited places are available for this service so it is advisable to book in advance.

There is truly something for everyone, no matter what your level of fitness may be. There is, for instance, a range of classes which offer workouts to music, the opportunity to develop a strong cardiovascular system, burn a few extra calories and meet new friends all at the same time.

The Dolphin Centre continues to be at the forefront of fitness provisions in Darlington. September 2001 saw an £80,000 investment in Pulse Suite II. This included thirty new pieces of state of the art fitness equipment, six wide screen televisions and a new reception area.

In addition, the latest health craze has been using stationary bikes for group cycling classes known as 'Spinning'! A dedicated spinning studio was created to meet the demands of this popular pastime allowing the public to experience an outdoor cycling session, indoors, no matter what the weather. Fully qualified staff motivate the customers with the latest training techniques and upbeat music.

Should you feel in need of a glimpse of the sun, there is no need to spend time and money on an expensive holiday abroad, simply go and enjoy a session on one of the sunbeds on offer.

In October 2002 the Dolphin Centre will have been open for twenty years. A historical occasion and no doubt many people who visited as children now visit as young adults, will continue to use the facilities in the future and will probably bring their children and grandchildren to do the same. The Dolphin Centre has made an enormous contribution to the fitness and enjoyment of the people of Darlington. Long may it continue to do so.

Top: Fun in the swimming pool.
Above: A concert performed at the Dolphin Centre.

In the frame

See a bare wall and we cannot wait to fill the space with a picture. Students and teenagers are in the habit of sticking a poster of their favourite pop star directly on to the wallpaper and fail to think ahead to the day comes when the icon of the day falls out of favour and the picture is taken down leaving those annoying bits of torn wallpaper as a permanent reminder of the otherwise forgotten hero. As we get older, wiser and more sophisticated our desire to fill our walls with images remains however just as strong. That urge is an ancient one, cavemen (and dare we say it cavewomen) painted directly on to the walls of their homes. The Romans too painted directly on to the walls of their houses. Here in Britain, from the time of the renaissance onwards, the wealthy aristocracy filled their homes with paintings by the great artists of the day but it was the Victorians who created enough wealth, spread over all sections of society, which increased the demand for paintings, etchings, and photographs a thousandfold.

By late Victorian times no home was complete without at least one picture and many, to judge from photographs of the period, seemed incomplete without every available wall space crammed with framed pictures both large and small. That fashion extended into public buildings too with our town halls and company board rooms hung with fine portraits of the great and the good.

But a picture is not a picture until it is framed. An artist completes his work when the paint is dry but the product is still not ready to be hung. The painted canvas must first be mounted in a suitable frame, one which matches the scale and theme of the canvass, one which matches the ultimate setting and one which is ideally as well crafted as the picture itself. To meet that demand the trade of picture framer came into being.

Above: *A manufacturers label.*
Below: *The William Dodds premises on Tubwell Row.*

glass and card with the framer's skill enhancing an artist's work if done well - and if done badly detract from it; no wonder those who owned pictures actively sought out a firm which could consistently add to a pictures aesthetic qualities. The art and skill of picture framing was essentially a craft which relied on patiently learned skills and the use of hand tools, some progress and modernisation however inevitably made its way into the craft as much as any other: in 1952 a Morso Mitre office machine was purchased, one of the first in the country. This helped speed up work. That machine is still in use along with other machinery which helps to produce the high quality work that is done today.

Now located at 34 Tubwell Row Darlington's longest established firm of specialist picture framers and fine art dealers, WM Dodds, has been a feature of the town since 1884. It was in that year that William Dodds, helped by his two brothers, began the picture framing firm which would be run by five generations of the family. The firm's present proprietor is the great grandson of the eponymous William.

In the firm's early days the business was based in Kendrew Street but demand for picture frames increased so much with the public's growing interest in art that the firm soon had to move to larger premises.

In 1961 the gallery was modernised and enlarged. Today, after well over a century the business continues, still specialising in picture framing and stocks a large selection of traditional and modern art for sale to home owners and commercial customers. Thousands of years after man first discovered art our interest, far from waning, remains, it seems, as strong as ever.

The present building in Tubwell Row was built to accommodate the long length of picture mouldings, some 12 feet long, which were stored upstairs. Most of the moulding for picture frames was bought from Cologne in Germany. The firm still has some of that early moulding still in its original wrappings and bearing its manufacturers' labels.

Above: *Part of the gallery .*
Below: *Tony Dodds.*

During the first decades of business a lot of the work produced was supplied to hang in municipal buildings, museums and town halls in the region.

Picture framing is an art in itself, the materials used include wood,

A cutting edge

Harry Boggon's interest in engineering started at a very early age. Born the youngest of seven children in Aldam Street, Darlington in 1920, Harry would follow his father and brothers who all worked for British Rail in having a keen interest in engineering and railways.

In 1950 Harry Boggon who at the time worked in North Road workshops, spent every spare minute of his time in his garden workshop in Cobden Street. There he manufactured circular saws and greenhouses, and carried out any machining work which came his way, he was known to family and friends as 'the workaholic'. As a keen amateur boxer Harry even managed to put aside a little time each week to pass his knowledge and dedication of the sport on to young people, teaching boxing at Borough Road Youth Centre.

Harry was offered a contract to manufacture components for blast furnaces in 1953 and he left British Rail, took on two men, and started his own precision engineering business. In 1963 premises owned by friends of Harry, CN Hadley Limited, became vacant in Harris Street, Darlington and North View Engineering was formed.

Over the following years Harry was joined in business by two of his children. North View Engineering became a private registered company in 1973. It soon began offering a much wider range of services to its customers including precision machining, in-house/on site maintenance and haulage to local industry. During annual shutdowns at local companies such as Patons and Baldwins and DSRM, North View would move in and carry out maintenance and refurbishment to the machinery and plant.

No job was too small, and they realised the need to react to clients' problems and to work non-stop to meet delivery deadlines. This approach is still applied today by Harold's younger son Jonathan the current Managing Director and daughter Patricia Hawes the Financial Director.

With demand for its products growing by the week the decision was taken in 1985 to move the firm to larger premises; these were found at its present location - Goldings

Above left: *Founder Harold Boggon with one of the first overspeed/overwind controllers, 1960.*
Below: *Harris Street machine shop in 1967.*

By the year 2000 the company was being asked to carry out more and more work for the Offshore, Steel, Chemical, Construction and Manufacturing industries, and in 2001 their second fabrication facility was opened enabling them to look forward to a bigger and brighter future.

Today North View Engineering Limited remains a dedicated family business and although it has developed its services and product range, it aims to still give each and every customer personal attention, service and commitment at all times. That philosophy has made the company what it is today - THE COMPLETE ENGINEERING PACKAGE.

Works, on Darlington's Cleveland Trading Estate. The additional space was soon taken up and further expansion was necessary. The company bought a number of bigger lathes and vertical and horizontal boring machines with increased capacity enabling them to cope with larger components, bought extra land and built their first fabrication facility.

Harry officially retired in 1985 and spent more time sailing his Hunter on Lake Ullswater.

Sadly in 1994 Harry died leaving the company to his children. It was obvious that Jonathan and Patricia had the same attitude and commitment to the business as their father and further development plans were soon being laid. The company was still growing and in order to maintain that growth additional staff were required. It was at this time that Paul Howard joined the firm and was soon to become a company director. Combining the traditional business policies laid down by Harry with the enthusiasm of this new management team proved to be a potent mixture.

This lead to new ambitions and achievements; by 1996 the company had become the 33rd fastest growing company in all sectors in the North East. With increased sales figures of 130 per cent over the previous financial year the company was also listed as being the tenth fastest growing company measured on sales growth.

Top: Work on the 300 ton structure on the Humber Sea Terminal. Above: Pontypridd Railway Station foot bridge, 2000. Below: The opening of a new Fabrication Workshop by Stephen Hughes MEP, (from left to right) Jonathan Boggon (Managing Director), Connie Boggon (founder's wife), Stephen Hughes (MEP), Patricia Hawes (Financial Director) and Paul Howard (Director).

The number one club

Snooker and socialising, bingo and beer, pie, peas and pop music. Working men's clubs may offer all of these, but the history of such clubs reaches back even further than these now time-honoured pleasures might suggest.

The Working Men's Club and Institute Union was founded on 14th June 1862 by the Reverend Henry Soly. Though generations have grown up to think of the working men's club movement as being a distinctly northern phenomenon the CIU had its roots in the South of England.

In Darlington, a little over a century ago a few railwaymen opened the campaign for the creation of a working men's club to be affiliated with the London-based Club and Institute Union. The result would be the first CIU club in Darlington - the Darlington Club and Institute, still located at 85 High Northgate and opened some twelve years before the second local club - the Houghton Working Men's Club.

The first formal meeting of those hoping to establish a club was held in Frarey's Cocoa Rooms, Tubwell Road on 1st March 1901. At the meeting a club president, secretary, treasurer and committee were appointed. The secretary was instructed to get into communication with Mr BT Hall the secretary of the Club and Institute Union who visited Darlington and supplied the committee members with model rules, books and literature on the working and management of such enterprises.

Several meetings of the committee were held in private houses. Various properties in the town were looked at which were likely to be suitable to house a club. The High Terrace property in High Northgate was vacant at the time and a deputation was appointed to negotiate with the owner, a Mr Hobson of Grange Road; but he would not agree to lease the property to the club, though he was prepared to sell.

Above: Darlington Northgate Club committee of 1926.
Bottom: The Darlington Club in 1926.

The 25th Anniversary of the club arrived with celebrations taking place from 6th-10th November 1926.

By then what still looked like any other Victorian terraced house had in place of the usual drawing rooms and sitting rooms, a games room and a billiard room; downstairs was a plush smoking room and a library crammed with books and daily papers: only the refreshment room looked vaguely like the haunt of a beer drinker.

Between then and the club's half centenary major alterations were made to the front of the club which made it into a far more imposing building.

The Jubilee was celebrated from Monday 5th November 1951 for 14 days. Since that jubilee many other structural alterations have taken place such as the removal of the 'cubicles', and relocation of the bar. The 1960s saw a large extension built to facilitate the construction of a 200 seat concert hall.

The club has survived more than 100 years thanks to the diligence of the members of its board of management, the tremendous support of members and associates and the help and guidance of the Club and Institute Union.

The next 100 years will see many new challenges, however with the support of members the committee believes they can be faced with confidence.

Lacking capital themselves the deputation then approached Mr J Foster, the club's first secretary. J Foster bought the property himself and made arrangements for the club to take over the premises at its convenience and on its terms.

The first committee meeting held on the club premises took place on 16th June 1901. At that meeting several of the first committee members who had been appointed were struck off because of non attendance and others were co-opted to take their places.

Then began the work of making alterations to the structure, furnishing it and registering the club, all of which took several months to complete. The official opening took place on 6th November 1901, the ceremony being performed by Herbert Pike Pease MP, later Lord Daryngton.

During the first 25 years of its life the club had to defend itself against oppressors. In 1903 it had to protect against trespass on its property, a question which was decided in the courts in Durham in the club's favour. In 1907 the club found itself up against the Darlington Assessment Committee, but again the courts at Durham found in its favour.

Top left: The Club's library, 1920s.
Above left: The committee of 1956.
Bottom: The Darlington Club and committee, 2001.

Quality sales and service

Alan H Goodrick founded his company in 1966. Alan, who was a qualified television service engineer opened his first shop in Northallerton in 1966, followed shortly afterwards with a shop on North Road, Darlington in the following year. On a dealer trip in 1987 to Portugal, Alan met a fellow dealer, Brian McPherson who during conversation discovered that Alan wished ultimately to retire from the business. The upshot of this meeting resulted in Brian being offered the position of General manager of Alan H Goodrick Ltd.

In 1995, Brian and his wife Margaret, who also worked for the company in administration, purchased the business. They had been with the firm eight years by this time and had played a major role in the daily routine and they were in admiration with the forward-looking stance of the company.

After 52 years in the industry, Alan retired a proud man after 30 years building up his company to be the acknowledged leading independent firm in Darlington; the Northallerton branch had closed in 1990.

Right: *David Everitt, Service Engineer, carrying out repairs.* **Bottom:** *Alan H Goodrick Ltd premises in North Road.*

For a large number of years, the company has been a member of 'Retra', the Radio Electrical Television Retailers Association, which has a membership of over 1500 retailers in the UK and in 1998, the company received an accolade when Brian, with 32 years experience in the industry, was elected President. The company always complies with the Association's strict code of practice which is of considerable benefit to its customers.

There is an in-house service department known locally as Goodricolour Service which undertakes a wide range of commissions from installing public address systems in restaurants and public houses to carrying out contract service for three multiple High Street retailers.

By selling quality products such as Panasonic, Sony and Loewe, the company has enabled its service installation technicians to gain extensive experience on projection TV and plasma technology. On washing machines and dishwashers they continue to install to a

The company expanded operations in 1999 and a Digital Home Cinema Shop was opened directly across from its North Road main showroom in Thompson Street East. Here you can see all the latest equipment concerned with hi-fi and home cinema equipment from brand leaders such as Yamaha, Panasonic, Technics, Sony and Denon.

Brian and Margaret's son, Stuart, works in the new outlet giving daily demonstrations on Home Cinema Digital Equipment such as DVD and digital prologic systems. Stuart's involvement with the company strengthens the family commitment to the firm's success in the future.

high standard as they do with refrigeration branded products such as Miele, Hotpoint and Bosch. Service and repair work to TV, video and hi-fi equipment is carried out in the company's fully equipped workshop on North Road.

The company is now a member of C I Holdings, which is now affiliated to Euronics, Europe's largest independent buying group and this ensures the customer is guaranteed competitive retail prices.

Displaying quality products competitively priced and offering strong service and installation support gives Alan H Goodrick Ltd the edge over their competitors. With the convergence of technologies the company believes they can offer a wide range of experience to guide customers in making the right choice for their own viewing or household requirements.

To accommodate the change in shopping habits that have become evident over recent times they have altered their opening hours and now open Monday to Friday 9am to 5.30pm, Saturday 9am to 5pm and Sunday 12 noon to 4pm. There is free daily parking outside the main showroom for customers. Adapting to new forms of shopping has also meant the acquisition of the company website; this can be visited at www.goodrick.co.uk.

Having two shops gives Alan H Goodrick the capability to quickly change direction in step with today's rapidly changing markets.

Alan H Goodrick Ltd would like to thank all their loyal customers who have supported the company over the last 36 years. As to the future, the company will continue to implement the aims of the founder in providing only top quality products, backed up by prompt in-house after sales service and above all - complete customer satisfaction.

Top and above left: *Views inside the showrooms.*
Bottom: *Alan H Goodrick Ltd premises in Thompson Street East.*

A switched on company forging ahead

It was during the 1880s that Henry Williams, who already held a number of patents, started his first works in Polmadie, Glasgow, the initial production being mainly of his own patent articles. About a year after this he invented the first spring railway switch lever for railway points. Previously all switches had been held in position by means of a weighted lever, and this first spring lever for track points and one way sidings was a marked improvement.

On the death of Henry Williams in 1899 the business was carried on by his four sons, Harry, Llewellyn, Owen and Denis. The business was incorporated in 1905, Owen became a very active chairman and displayed an enthusiasm and a drive for the business which played a very large part in the success of the firm.

By 1911, the expansion of the business warranted a move and Darlington was chosen, as it had the advantage of proximity to the railway network. The firm acquired its present-day site at this time and supplied the many railway companies with the company's products in large quantities. Their markets were chiefly in the UK, but not exclusively so. During the second decade of the century, the firm undertook the supply of the complete signalling requirements of the Colombo Peradeniya line in Ceylon.

During the First World War, the expansion of the railway and Permanent Way and signalling items had to be curtailed, to concentrate on the manufacture of limber hooks for guns, general service wagons for field kitchens and various types of bombs mostly for trench mortars and similar weapons.

At the end of the war signalling manufacture resumed and expanded in the 1920s. A large number of items were manufactured in Darlington and exported. A considerable

Above left: *Founder Henry Williams.*
Bottom: *Mr & Mrs Denis Williams (centre) pictured with staff.*

In March, 1989, Henry Williams Ltd was bought by the Con Mech Group, who, for ease of operation divided the production facility into two separate manufacturing companies with a total workforce of around 100. The forge and fabrication section became Henry Williams Darlington Ltd and the electrical facility, Henry Williams Electrical Ltd. Until this point, the company had been owned and managed by three generations of the Williams family, spanning the previous 106 years.

The privatisation of the railways brought new challenges for Henry Williams Electrical Ltd and their services are also in demand in the water, nuclear power and petro-chemical industries. A highly skilled workforce operates from the original site in Darlington but can now be found almost anywhere in the UK installing, commissioning and maintaining their electrical assemblies and railway signalling systems.

The Henry Williams Darlington operation has a reputation for quality and service that is worthy of their pedigree. They do not rest on their past reputation however, but continue to invest in technology which will keep them at the forefront of design and manufacturing techniques. They have an unwavering commitment to quality, a fact endorsed by the ISO 9000 approval they have achieved.

Today the company has developed into a versatile and multi-skilled engineering business, using their traditional skills and expertise to manufacture a diverse range of forgings for the demanding applications of the engineering industry. In addition to its long standing involvement with railways, new products are being produced for the nation's motorways and bridges.

Top left: A 62ft Signal Gantry built for Ryhope Grange, North Eastern Region. *Above left:* Henry Williams Signalling Equipment on show at a Railway Exhibition in 1959. *Below:* Celebrating the Centenary of Henry Williams Ltd, 1983.

proportion of this trade went to India and the firm opened a branch works in Calcutta.

During the second world war, the firm developed a new method of producing trench mortar bombs which saved 30 per cent of the steel required previously. This was achieved through greater accuracy and a reduced amount of machining required. Altogether 2 million of these bombs were made and by the end of the war, the Darlington works had made a total of over seven million forgings for munitions.

The Williams family believed in carrying on Henry's tradition and were actively engaged in the management and technical development of the firm's products. In 1937 Owen's son, Tony, joined the firm but not until he had finished his studies at Cambridge and had spent two years on a pupillage in the Permanent Way and Signalling Departments of the LMS railway and then in one of the leading motor firms to complete his training.

New plant was installed after the end of the Second World War and continued to supply the railway industry with a unique service which brought together the firm's expertise in forging and machining, resulting in a high quality and cost-effective product.

Assisting an active and independant retirement

The Darlington Abbeyfield Society was set up in 1970 by a joint committee of the Darlington Rotary Club and the Soroptimist Club. The soroptimists were considering what to do with a fund established by their founder president, Miss Nora Fenby, and it was this money, together with other sums raised by the Rotary Club, that enabled the Society to make a start.

Nora Fenby was Headmistress of Eastbourne Girls' Secondary School, Darlington at her retirement in 1963. She started her teaching career at Loftus and taught at several schools in the Cleveland area before going to Goldsmiths College, London from 1918 to 1920. She was appointed to Sandford Girls' School, Guildford, Surrey in 1920 and remained there until 1923 when she returned to her native city to teach at Beaumont Street Girls' School. She moved to the new Eastbourne Senior Girls' School in 1963.

The Abbeyfield Society is part of a national organisation. There are over 800 Houses in the UK run by some 600 Abbeyfield Societies providing family style living for those elderly people who are no longer able or willing to live alone, but who wish to

live an independent life. Each House has separate en-suite accommodation for about nine residents with a resident Housekeeper to keep an eye on things and to provide the two main meals a day.

Understandably there is a waiting list for places in these Houses. Residents are selected from applicants who meet the society's criteria on being elderly, active and lonely. The method and procedure of selection is designed to ensure that all applicants are dealt with fairly having regard to their individual needs. Applications are received by the honorary secretary from individuals either direct or by referral from the Local Authority and other agencies such as the Citizens' Advice Bureau and the housing Aid Centre.

When a vacancy occurs, and in any event, at regular intervals, the waiting list is reviewed. Approval of the applicant is by decision of a sub-committee of the Executive Committee after considering all the necessary information - this includes a personal interview.

Above: Nora Fenby.
Below: Nora Fenby House, the first Abbeyfield House.

Once accepted, the resident must pay the weekly charge and comply with a simple set of rules to ensure the comfort and well-being of the residents as a whole. In return the resident has the right to treat his or her room as they would their own home - to come and go as they please, to have friends and relatives to visit them and to take part in whatever activities they wish, either in or out of the House.

Guest rooms are available at the Houses and prospective residents are encouraged to stay in one of these for a week so that they can establish whether 'Abbeyfield life' is for them.

Abbeyfield rooms are intended for the fit and active and nursing facilities are not provided. Residents needing that kind of care vacate their rooms allowing the opportunities of living in an Abbeyfield House to be taken up by someone else.

Darlington's first Abbeyfield House, Nora Fenby House, was opened in 1974. It is in a delightful setting with a view across the Green towards St Mary's Church, Cockerton. Lady Starmer,

who was at the opening in 1974, was so impressed that she bequeathed her home, Danby Lodge and its extensive grounds, to the society. She was a lady of outstanding kindness and generosity, asking only that it be named after her late husband, Sir Charles Starmer, who had been a former Mayor and Alderman of Darlington, a Member of Parliament and founder of the North of England Newspaper Company, forerunner of the Westminster Press.

Lady Starmer died in 1979 and the funeral service had to be relayed to the 'overspill' assembled in the church hall, such was the number of people who wished to pay their last respects. The Northern Echo, reporting the event described Lady Starmer as Darlington's best-loved citizen. Lord Ramsey, former Archbishop of Canterbury spoke of her as 'a wonderful person, a wonderful Christian and a wonderful friend'.

Above: Lady Starmer pictured in 1967 and her husband Sir Charles Starmer during his first spell as Mayor of Darlington, 1907-1908. Below: Danby Lodge, the former home of Lady and Sir Charles Starmer, now an Abbeyfield House.

With the help of a Housing Corporation Grant and Public Appeal, Sir Charles Starmer House was converted and opened in December 1982 to another nine residents, a Housekeeper and her husband.

Miss Muriel Latimer was a friend of Lady Starmer and daughter of the late John Fenwick Latimer, a leading Darlington Solicitor, Alderman and colleague of Sir Charles Starmer. Miss Latimer was so pleased at the conversion of Sir Charles Starmer House that she left the residue of her considerable estate to the society in memory of her father. Miss Latimer was educated at Polam Hall School in Darlington and studied ballet in Darlington before joining the Lydia Kyasht's Russian Ballet. She later became a ballet teacher in the Darlington area. In making her bequest to the society she said it was meant to be, 'an expression of [her father's] concern and affection for the inhabitants of Darlington'.

After failing to find a suitable property it was decided to commission a purpose-built residence to be called J F Latimer House in the grounds of Danby Lodge. This house was opened in 1986. With the remaining part of Miss Latimer's bequest, together with funds from Thomas Earl and Miss Keelan, the Society was able to build Earl Keelan House on the same site in 1990.

These well-known Darlington personalities and benefactors have enabled many elderly people to live in four friendly happy houses. They are not 'old people's homes' but affordable family sized Houses providing a careful combination of independence with support and provide with companionship. Thanks to Nora Fenby, Sir Charles and lady Starmer, Miss Muriel and JF Latimer, Thomas Earl and Miss Keelan, a helpful Local Authority and many dedicated hardworking volunteers, Darlington Abbeyfield Society has been able to provide housing care of a high standard for nearly thirty years.

The Darlington Abbeyfield Society Limited is a non-profit-making company. It is a registered with the charity Commission as a Charity and with the Housing Corporation as such is required to conform to the Corporation's high standards. It is affiliated to The Abbeyfield Society and a member of the Independent Housing Ombudsman Scheme.

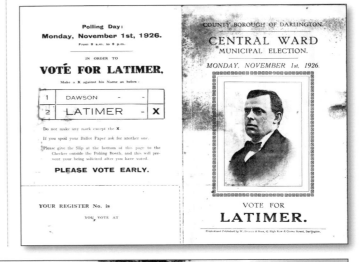

Top left: Muriel Latimer.
Above right: A JF Latimer election leaflet from 1926. **Right**: *Latimer House.*
Below: *Earl Keelan House.*

First quarry past the post

The expression a 'self made man' is a rare accolade. One man who certainly has earned that title is John Wade the owner of John Wade (Haulage) Ltd based at the Aycliffe Quarry and also Stonegrave Aggregates Ltd which has invested £millions in recent years to wrest more than half a million tonnes of limestone from the earth each year.

John Wade lives locally on one of his farms where, in addition to farming a considerable area of arable land and breeding Limousin Cattle, trains his own impressive stable of racehorses. He has also served as the Master of the South Durham Hunt.

Sedgefield Racecourse, where John is a director, has seen him in the winners' enclosure many times but arguably his finest hours have been at Cheltenham: in 1999 and 2000 where John's horse Overflowing River won the Cheltenham Hunters four mile steeplechase.

It sounds an idyllic life but in 1958, when at the age of fifteen John Wade left school, he could hardly have anticipated being a successful businessman and race horse owner. His first job was at the Tees Agricultural Engineers at Blands Corner - on the site of what would later become Reg Vardy Car Showrooms. John's first wage packet back then was a mere 10 3/4 d per hour - just £2 per week.

When John was nineteen or so he began repairing and driving earth moving plant. He worked on the construction of the A1(M) Darlington by-pass in 1963 being a driver/fitter for Alan Blair of Darlington. John's next move was to Elliott's Earthmoving, gaining more experience on civil engineering sites.

In 1964, John started out on his own as an agricultural engineer. That fledgling enterprise would quickly move into plant hire and small contract work involving earth moving re-seeding and demolition.

Those early activities soon progressed into quarry products sales as John became a merchant, collecting stone from the Old Town Quarry at Middridge near Shildon and delivering it to local builders and councils.

Above: *Founder, John Wade pictured in 1962.*
Below: *Aycliffe Quarry.*

In 1972 John Wade was able to buy the firm of Stonegrave Aggregates Ltd based at the Aycliffe Quarry from Maurice Francis, a local businessman who lived in Woodland Road Darlington. John soon initiated changes by scrapping the by now disused kilns that had previously supplied burnt/calcined dolomite used to produce high temperature insulation and pharmaceuticals to the Chemical & Insulating Company at Faverdale, Darlington .

Other outlets were needed. John expanded the quarry and was soon supplying the construction industry with crushed dolomite - magnesium limestone for the technically minded. Many of the Darlington houses, factories and roads built in the last quarter of the 20th century were built on Aycliffe Quarry hardcore. Wimpy Homes in particular built many new family homes using John Wade's Aycliffe Quarry dolomite for their house bases, roads and sewers

Meanwhile the demolition and reclamation side of the business flourished with several large contracts in Darlington. Such work for example included the demolition and site clearance of the old Stephenson and Hawthorn Engine Works off Thompson Street in 1985. (Latterley it had become the Phoenix Tubeman Works) Again, this site was transformed into a new housing development.

Another demolition project was the Cleveland Bridge and Engineering Works in Smithfield Road. The land reclamation and removal of contaminated earth at that site would provide land for many new homes. Today families are living on the site where famous bridges were

manufactured, like the Firth of Forth in Scotland and Sidney Harbour in Australia.

The old Salvation Army hostel at the corner of Haughton Road and St Cuthbert's Way, a well known local landmark, disappeared almost overnight in 1987 thanks to John Wade. This large Victorian hostel was demolished in a single weekend, with John Wade completely clearing the site of 2,000 tons of rubble and giving commuters a surprise new view as they travelled into town on the Monday morning. The site is now occupied by modern, elegant offices.

During the 1990s John expanded taking on larger earth moving demolition and land reclamation work regionally but mostly in and around the Darlington area.

Top: *The demolition of the Stephenson & Hawthorn Engine Works, 1985.* **Above right:** *Demolition of outdated council houses.*

Often demolition contracts were followed up by successfully winning work to excavate for new buildings on the site, again utilising stone from the Aycliffe Quarry.

In 1995 he acquired Selset Quarry located near Selset reservoir, a few miles from Middleton in Teesdale, increasing the range and quality of stone available. Today over 100,000 tonnes of carboniferous blue limestone are extracted from here each year: some which has been used for sea defence contracts and flood prevention on the River Tees.

It is also fair to say that the name of John Wade is synonymous with local transport as his wagons can be regularly observed on many roads throughout the North East

As a quarry owner John is one of the few independents left in the mineral extraction industry dominated by the like of Tarmac and Lafarge. In the North East John Wade is a force to be reckoned with giving high quality service and prices that are hard if not impossible to beat. The Wade quarries attract much important business, not least when Stonegrave was able to supply all the roadstone, a quarter of a million tonnes during 1997 and 1998, for an extra lane on the A19 motorway that passes through Teesside.

At the turn of the new millennium the John Wade empire has directly employed about 140 local people but many more jobs were also supported as a result of buying goods and services and also the purchases of lorries, earth moving machines, fuel, tyres, crushers and cars that are necessary for John Wade's extensive activities.

Today John Wade (Haulage) Ltd and Stonegrave Aggregates Ltd offer clients a wide range of services such as wagon hire, skip collection and waste disposal. Tipping facilities are available at Aycliffe Quarry where Stonegrave Aggregates holds a licence to dispose of construction waste. Demolition contracting continues with the ball and chain replaced by a fleet of mechanised hydraulic machines which can cut their way through the toughest concrete. Plant hire forms an integral part of the business with an ever widening range of equipment available including 360 degree excavators, dozers and dump trucks.

The firm recently carried out civil engineering contract work for the Wynyard Cycle Way which in 2001 was officially opened by Prime Minister Tony Blair.

With enough hard work and application a man can make his own luck. In John Wade's case that has worked in business and in pleasure - there is no reason why this should not continue for many years to come.

Top, both pictures: *Part of The John Wade fleet.*
Left: *John Wade being presented with the Winners Magnum of Champagne by Pat Pheonix (Elsie Tanner of Coronation Street fame) after his success at Cartmel Races with 'Son of Monardo'.*

A *taste of the good things in life*

Bread; crusty rolls, soft rolls, wholemeal bread, fruit bread, large white tins, bloomers, granary loaves, brown cobs, farmhouse loaves; bread, the staff of life, how would we live without it? We would undoubtedly survive but would be hard pressed to find a substitute for the sheer variety and versatility of this humble flour, yeast and water mixture which is capable of being both a comfort food and an item of great luxury.

Bread has been around for centuries, since a certain Chinese Ching-Noung taught men the method of making bread from wheat, and ever since bread has been an important part of life for people all over the world. Of course not all bread is of the same quality. Anyone who has tasted bread made by a skilled baker, whether produced at home or in a specialist bakery will scarcely feel able to call the mass-produced doughy product produced in humid steam tunnels and transported miles before getting to the supermarket shelves by the same name.

Bakers, using traditional skills, are possibly the last of the many one-man businesses still to produce the products of their craft by using local knowledge of what is required and traditional skills. Bread was first made with yeast by English master bakers in 1634 and in the mid-1800s a Doctor Daughlish patented a method of making bread with a mixture of aerated water and flour - the forerunner of what we now know as soda bread.

In this illustrious tradition stands a Darlington family, the Kershaws. This

local family bakery has been producing high quality bread and confectionery at The Leas' Bakery for the people of Darlington for over forty years.

It was in August 1960 that Norman and Elizabeth Kershaw set up in business in The Leas'. Norman had served in the Royal Navy to start with and later he managed a bakery in Bates Avenue, Darlington. Together the couple went into a business of their own, making use of their skills and enthusiasm for quality products made by hand. In the early days Norman ran the bakery and Elizabeth served in the shop, building up relationships with their loyal customers.

All the products in a baker's shop have to be made fresh each day and they have to be available when shoppers come out to buy; it means therefore that early mornings come as part of the job description, and like everything else about which you have no choice, it eventually becomes an accepted part of life. Once the day's baking was over, Norman set about delivering

Above: *Norman (left) and Ken with Norman's eldest Grandson Ben in the background, aged four at the time, Ben is now twenty.* **Right:** *Leas Bakery at the start of the 21st century.*

There were a couple of memorable times in the 1970s when there were bread strikes. There was no bread at all in the supermarkets and people had to get bread from wherever they could. So the Kershaws and others like them were inundated with potential customers seeking to buy as much as they could. On one occasion they had someone come to the shop who offered to buy their entire day's production. Such times made heavy demands and necessitated Ken and Norman to work 18 hour days. Of course at such times it was the regular customers who were given priority when supplies were running low.

regular orders to customers who couldn't get to the shop. This is a truly valuable service for those who find it difficult to get out and many looked forward to taking delivery of aromatic freshly baked bread and delicious cakes which Norman brought to their doors. It is interesting that supermarkets seem just to be coming round to this idea - at last.

This policy was proved to be the right one, since many who were so grateful to buy the Kershaw's bread during the strike immediately went back to the supermarket once the strikes were over.

Today it is the second generation of Kershaws who are getting up early to stock the bakery shelves. Norman and Elizabeth's eldest son, Ken and his wife, Joy now

The main competition to the Kershaws as well as to all other privately owned businesses selling food of any description is, and for some time has been, the supermarkets. These large chains can offer the whole variety of food items but are unable to compete in terms of freshness and variety of goods offered and the service provided by the small family run business. Many appreciate this and the Kershaws certainly have many satisfied and loyal customers who wouldn't think about buying bread and cakes from anywhere else.

Top left: *Norman after the shop refit in 1986.*
Right: *Liz, Joy and Allison in the shop.*

on the fine reputation which has been built up over the last forty or more years. The Kershaws have been greatly assisted in their business by a hard-working and loyal staff without whom they could not have accomplished all they have managed to do.

Perhaps the only thing which would threaten the future of a bakery like The Leas' Bakery is if bread should somehow go out of fashion. The proven health benefits of good quality bread and the enthusiasm with which it is bought by every family would suggest that this is extremely unlikely. Nor in these health and weight conscious days does it seem at all conceivable that the demand for freshly baked cakes is about to dry up. The Leas' Bakery can look forward to many prosperous days ahead.

run the bakery. Ken worked alongside his mother in the shop for many years before being initiated into the ancient craft of baking.

Over the years certain things have changed. At the start every single item was hand-made, nowadays the Kershaws permit themselves the convenience of food mixers and fridges but still maintain the valued tradition of making most things by hand.

The bakery has always been at the present site in The Leas' but is somewhat larger than when Norman and Elizabeth started out. Extra space has been acquired by extending the original premises. Some years ago in 1986, the bakery and shop underwent a substantial refit and now consists of a convenient and well-planned bakery section and an attractive shop area.

The Kershaws are justly proud of their achievement in serving the local community by providing an extensive range of high quality baked products and their plan is to continue to do so in the future, building

Above: Norman and Elizabeth Kershaw.
Below: Joy and Ken Kershaw.

Ambition, determination and gain

For nearly 130 years, Amdega of Faverdale industrial estate, Darlington, have been making fine timber conservatories, combining Victorian grace with the latest technology. These days conservatories are extremely popular but not many people realise that the concept of a structure made of glass which let light in but kept the frost out dates back to the time when Sir Walter Raleigh brought exotic plans from his world travels which needed warmer surroundings than were generally on offer in this country's climate.

Conservatories began to catch on in the domestic realm after the Crystal Palace was built to house the 1851 Great Exhibition and many wealthy householders sought to recreate scaled down versions of this for their homes.

Before long everybody wanted one and William Richardson & Company was established in Darlington in 1874 to take advantage of the new fashion by constructing greenhouses and vineries for commercial growers and private houses.

Demand for their high quality product continued to increase throughout the 20th century, with two breaks for the two World Wars. During the first world war Richardsons were able to put their skill in producing high quality joinery to good use in manufacturing biplane parts for the Royal Flying Corps, aeroplanes being at the time made largely of wood. During the second world war they manufactured sheds and other temporary buildings which were not only quick to erect but strong and substantial enough to withstand the wide ranging demands made on them.

Timber was in short supply after the war so Richardsons began producing greenhouses with aluminium frames. Once the Armed Forces were demobbed and life gradually returned to normal there was a substantial increase in the demand for commercial greenhouses and conservatories.

The turning point came in 1963 when a change to the company's name was decided upon. The word Amdega was coined from 'ambition', 'determination' and 'gain' which reflected the qualities on which the company had been built. There was a rebirth of the fashion for domestic conservatories at this time and Amdega rapidly established itself as the leading company in the field, a position it retains to this day.

Above: A William Richardson & Company Conservatory, early 1900s. **Below left:** *An Amdega conservatory from the 1940s.* **Below:** *A recent example of a fine Amdega conservatory.*

Crowds milling about the Market Place to celebrate Whit Monday in 1955.

Acknowledgments

The publishers would like to thank
Darlington Local Studies Library